PORNOGRAPHY AND SEXUAL VIOLENCE

Gary E. McCuen

IDEAS IN CONFLICT SERIES

publications inc.

411 Mallalieu Drive
Hudson, Wisconsin 54016

Illustration & photo credits
Chicago Tribune 59, The Guardian 86, Jack Hamm 22, 63, 106, The Militant 28, 36, 72, Minneapolis Star & Tribune 40, Morality In Media 12, National Coalition to Prevent Child Abuse 82, U.S.A. Today 90, Women Against Pornography Newsreport 17, 49, 116

©1985 by Gary E. McCuen Publications, Inc.
411 Mallalieu Drive ● Hudson, Wisconsin 54016 ●
(715) 386-5662
International Standard Book Number 0-86596-053-4
Printed in the United States of America

CONTENTS

CHAPTER 5   PORNOGRAPHY IN FOREIGN NATIONS: Global Perspectives

REASONING SKILL DEVELOPMENT

These activities may be used as individualized study guides for students in libraries and resource centers or as discussion catalysts in small group and classroom discussions.

IDEAS in CONFLICT ®

This series features ideas in conflict on political, social and moral issues. It presents counterpoints, debates, opinions, commentary and analysis for use in libraries and classrooms. Each title in the series uses one or more of the following basic elements:

Introductions that present an issue overview giving historic background and/or a description of the controversy.

Counterpoints and debates carefully chosen from publications, books, and position papers on the political right and left to help librarians and teachers respond to requests that treatment of public issues be fair and balanced.

Symposiums and forums that go beyond debates that can polarize and oversimplify. These present commentary from across the political spectrum that reflect how complex issues attract many shades of opinion.

A global emphasis with foreign perspectives and surveys on various moral questions and political issues that will help readers to place subject matter in a less culture-bound and ethno-centric frame of reference. In an ever shrinking and interdependent world, understanding and cooperation are essential. Many issues are global in nature and can be effectively dealt with only by common efforts and international understanding.

Reasoning skill study guides and discussion activities provide ready made tools for helping with critical reading and evaluation of content. The guides and activities deal with one or more of the following:

RECOGNIZING AUTHOR'S POINT OF VIEW

INTERPRETING EDITORIAL CARTOONS

VALUES IN CONFLICT

WHAT IS EDITORIAL BIAS?

WHAT IS SEX BIAS?

WHAT IS POLITICAL BIAS?

WHAT IS ETHNOCENTRIC BIAS?

WHAT IS RACE BIAS?

WHAT IS RELIGIOUS BIAS?

From across **the political spectrum** varied sources are presented for research projects and classroom discussions. Diverse opinions in the series come from magazines, newspapers, syndicated columnists, books, political speeches, foreign nations, and position papers by corporations and non-profit institutions.

About The Editor

Gary E. McCuen is an editor and publisher of anthologies for public libraries and curriculum materials for schools. Over the past 14 years his publications of over 200 titles have specialized in social, moral and political conflict. They include books, pamphlets, cassettes, tabloids, filmstrips and simulation games, many of them designed from his curriculums during 11 years of teaching junior and senior high school social studies. At present he is the editor and publisher of the *Ideas in Conflict* series and the *Editorial Forum* series.

CHAPTER 1

DEFINING PORNOGRAPHY
Values in Conflict

CHAPTER OVERVIEW

1 PORNOGRAPHY AS OBSCENITY
   Morality in Media

2 PORNOGRAHY AS RACIAL AND SEXUAL
   VIOLENCE
   Loretta Benjamin

3 A CHRISTIAN PERSPECTIVE
   American Lutheran Church

4 A SOCIALIST PERSPECTIVE ON
   PORNOGRAPHY
   Maggie McCraw

DEFINING PORNOGRAPHY:
Values in Conflict

Chapter Overview

The definition and regulation of pornography has been a difficult problem in Western nations where free speech is a central political tradition. Frederick Schauer in the **Encyclopedia of Crime and Justice** defines pornography as a "visual medium, achieving its effect by the words or pictures in books, magazines, motion pictures, television, videotape and the like." Pornography is traditionally thought of as a portrayal of sexual activity designed to promote sexual arousal. The pornography question has been a great national issue in the United States where the first amendment is often found to be in conflict with attempts to regulate pornography, frequently defined in legal and moral terms as obscenity.

The obscenity definition has more than legal problems, since the specific term obscene refers to something repulsive or offensive. A visual or written portrayal of sex could be obscene, but would not have to always be so. The opposite situation could also be true. Something considered obscene would not have to have anything to do with showing or describing sexual activity.

Though different groups argue over definitions and purpose, the producers, sellers, and consumers of pornography have a clear understanding of its meaning. For them it is a written or visual product showing sexual anatomy and/or sexual activity designed to promote sexual arousal. The terms "soft-core" and "hard-core" distinguish between two basic versions or types of pornography. Hard-core pornography is usually more detailed in descriptions and visual portrayals of sexual organs and activity. Its most distinguishing feature, however, is the merging of sexual activity with violent acts. Portrayals of rape, child molestation, sadism, and bestiality are commonplace in violent hard-core pornography. The so-called "snuff" films show scenes of women being raped, tortured, and murdered.

This chapter presents four different definitions of pornography. It is representative of how some social and political forces define pornography and its effect on our national life.

9

PORNOGRAPHY AS OBSCENITY
Morality in Media

Morality in Media defines itself as a non-profit, non-sectarian organization working to help stop traffic in pornography. It is concerned with helping communities express discontent with pornography and indecency in the media. Indecency is defined by the U.S. Supreme Court as "non-conformance with accepted standards of morality." (July 1978)

Points To Consider

1. How is pornography defined and what is the extent of the problem?
2. Why is pornography socially destructive?
3. What causes the widespread use of pornographic materials?
4. What is the solution to the problem?

Excerpted from a **Morality in Media** pamphlet, 1983.

Hard-core pornography, exhibited in films and magazines, has invaded every town, large and small, through so-called "adult" bookstores, "adult" theatres, and peep shows.

Yes, you can help turn the tide of pornography that is washing away the moral fabric of our society, corrupting our children, eating away at our family structure, physically destroying entire areas of our cities . . .

- With your voice
- With your pen
- With your telephone
- With your friends
- With Morality in Media, Inc.

The Problem—The traffic in pornography and obscenity has reached frightening proportions in this country. The smallest cities and towns have been invaded by it. There are almost 750 so-called "adult" movie houses in the country, showing the most obscene films imaginable. This is not counting the houses that show homosexual pornographic films exclusively. Many of the 750 sell casettes of hard-core movies in their lobbies. "Adult" bookstores are so numerous that it is almost impossible to count them on the national level. There is pornography going through the U.S. mails everyday. There are family service stores displaying and selling "men's" magazines in full view of and within browsing reach of children. The ideology of pornography—sex anywhere, any time, with anyone of any sex—is rampant on the commercial television screen. And, now, pornography is actually invading the living room on cable television. The problem is vast and it is taking its toll. But it doesn't have to be that way.

Solution

The solution lies in the law and in a vocal public urging continuous, vigorous enforcement of the law. There are federal, state and local laws that make it a crime to traffic in obscenity. The law is on the side of the people, not on the side of the pornographer. The Supreme Court repeated in 1973 that obscenity is NOT protected by the first amendment. The Court said at the same time that in determining whether material is obscene or not, COMMUNITY standards must be applied. But a judge or a jury can't know what those standards are if you, the community, do not *express* them. So, the solution is up to an *informed* and *vocal* community. That's where Morality in Media comes in . . .

11

"What is at stake is
civilization and humanity,
nothing less."

IRVING KRISTOL,
Henry R. Luce Professor of
Urban Values,
New York University

Morality in Media is a national organization working to stop the traffic in pornography constitutionally and effectively, and working for media based on love, truth and good taste. Morality in Media (MM) began and continues with two aims:
1. To alert and *inform* parents and community leaders about the extent of the traffic in pornography and its dangers, and
2. To encourage communities to express themselves in an informed, reasoned, continuous and unified way to: a. Law enforcement officials urging continuous and vigorous enforcement of obscenity laws and, b. to legitimate media makers, and sponsors urging responsibility in broadcasting. . .

A Destructive Social Ill

"It was those pornographic films," said a rapist in England as he was being sentenced to life imprisonment for seven rapes and an act of sodomy. He described the porn films' effect on him: "It was like living in hell, in another world. I just had to do something."

"It's outrageous," said a police official in an American city, "to permit an 'adult' book store to operate across the street from a school." A suspect in several child molestation cases, involving children in the school, had been reported seen in the book store.

Pornography is a 6 billion dollar a year racket. Hard-core pornography, exhibited in films and magazines, has invaded every town, large and small, through so-called "adult" bookstores, "adult" theatres, and peep shows. It is moving through the U.S. mails.

Even the local newsstand, drug store and grocery store have opened their doors to the sale of degrading materials.

The *ideology* of pornography is infecting the American family through the television screen: sex anytime, anywhere, with anyone of any sex.

And now the sex industry is fast moving into Cable television, invading our living rooms.

The pornography disease has reached epidemic proportions, and continues to spread.

Why?

1. Money. Profits are astronomical. A hard-core magazine, for example, sold in adult bookstores, costs 1.25 to 1.75 to produce and print. The bookstores charge $10 for the magazine. With profits like this, what happens? Organized crime moves in. Two grand juries have found that organized crime controls 90% of the hard-core pornography traffic in the country.
2. A heretofore quiet public. Lack of public expression is taken for toleration.
3. A lack of vigorous enforcement of obscenity law on the federal, state and local levels.

What Is It Doing To Us?

The visible effects are all too obvious. It is ravaging entire areas of our cities and towns; for, once a pornography outlet opens, it is followed by another, and another. The outlets breed other crime, such as prostitution and drug pushing, with the ultimate deterioration of the area.

But Even Worse:

Pornography is loveless; it is therefore an attack on the familial character of true human sexual expression, and so an attack on the family itself, the foundation on which our society is built.

Pornography undermines the moral fiber of the community and the nation. A nation that does not control pornography, and protect acceptable standards of public morality, does not survive.

Our families, our cities, our nation, our society are suffering with the disease of pornography.

But, it is not too late. There is a way to turn the tide.

Law Enforcement

The U.S. Supreme Court said in June of 1973: "This much has been categorically settled by the court, that obscene material is unprotected by the First Amendment." Obscenity is *not* protected by the First Amendment. It is a crime. There have been obscenity laws on the books since the founding of our nation. There are obscenity laws on the books now—federal laws, state laws and local ordinances.

The mere existence of the laws means nothing, however, unless they are enforced and enforced vigorously. Continuous, vigorous enforcement of obscenity laws on every level—federal, state, local—could see an end to the pornography plague within two years.

But, law enforcement officials—often overburdened and under-staffed—are not inclined to arrest and prosecute unless they hear the public voice. Your voice.

Your voice can help cure the disease of pornography that is destroying the moral, spiritual and cultural life of our country.

Your voice, raised with and channeled through organization can bring action on all levels: *federal, state, local.*

VALUES IN CONFLICT

PORNOGRAPHY AS RACIAL AND SEXUAL VIOLENCE
Loretta Benjamin

Loretta Benjamin is a member of Women for Racial and Economic Equality (WREE). Their publication is called the WREE-View. This article deals with the economic, racial, and sexual causes and effects of pornographic publications.

Points To Consider

1. What is the relationship between rape, sexual violence, and pornography?
2. How is racism related to pornography?
3. What have social scientists said about pornography and violence?

Loretta Benjamin, "The Porno Business," The WREE-View, publication of Women for Racial and Economic Equality. WREE-View is available at WREE's office at 130 E. 16th St., New York, N.Y. 10003.

The growing problem of rape is being fueled by the burgeoning pornography in the mainstream of American life.

Throughout history rape has been an accepted custom in certain instances, as in wartime when rape was often deemed a part of the spoils. There have always been people who see fit to describe their sexual enjoyments and fantasies for the titillation of others.

Today the combined force of rape and pornography is cutting a swathe through the already tattered fabric of understanding between men and women. Rape has reached crisis proportions; someone is raped in the United States every eight minutes, day and night, and women are the majority of the victims.

Half of all reported rapes are committed by assailants known to the victims. The majority of both victims and offenders are between the ages of 15 and 25, thus giving many parents and youth concern about dating experiences.

Rapes take place most often in the victim's home, and the second most common place is the assailant's home. Most rape victims are overcome without the use of a weapon; the threat of bodily harm forces compliance.

This last fact opens up one of the many gray areas concerning the use of force in connection with rape. Fear and threats are forms of force. Many people willingly comfort the victim if they see visible results of violence (cuts and bruises), but few extend sympathy to a victim who exhibits no outward sign of struggle.

Indeed, the conviction still prevails that a woman should gladly suffer death rather than rape, and many more blame the woman's attitude or dress for "provoking" the attack. However, most rapists give as reasons for the assault, the need to overpower and dominate. The dress or appearance of the victim has no bearing on the rapist's decision to attack.

Over the past 10 years, as the consciousness of women has been raised, more are willing to discuss and come to grips with their feelings about rape. These discussions have helped many women to dispel the myth that "nice girls don't get raped."

Racism And Sexism

Compounding the rampant sexist nature of pornography is the added element of racism. Many pornography films depict Black, Asian, and other minority women being sexually abused by white men. This reinforces the racist notion that minority women are "fair game" for the lusts of white men. This is of particular concern to Black women who have historically been

16

the victims of rape by white slaveowners, employers, and supervisors.

Indeed, the rape of Black women in the United States has been particularly cruel because the Black woman historically could not look to her husband or male relatives for protection. Often, Black men were forced to witness the abuse of their women, on pain of death if they tried to stop the rape.

Just as pornography has created the "fair game" policy for Black women, rape laws have been created to keep in check the mythical "rampaging Black rapist," who is out to sully the "virtue of white womanhood." This tool has been used to keep in "place" or eliminate many Black activists and otherwise "uppity" Black men.

In the past 40 years 455 men have been executed for the crime of rape: 405 were Black and 398 of the executions took place in the South. No white man has ever been executed in this country for raping a Black woman. A Philadelphia study has shown that the likelihood of any Black woman being raped by a white man is three times greater than the chance of any white woman being raped by a Black man.

The growing problem of rape is being fueled by the burgeoning pornography in the mainstream of American life. During the 70s the "sexual revolution" became popular fare for the mass media—literally an invasion of the family livingroom with material depicting women as objects to be exploited for the sexual pleasure of men.

Violence And Pornography

A large part of this pornographic blitz pairs sexual pleasure with violence and develops the concept that women are expendable. Countless plots for television dealing with rape, murder, kidnap, beating, and mayhem, done to the leading man's wife, girl friend, sister, mother, or acquaintance, became the rule in every action, adventure, or medical primetime show.

Similarly, pornography in movies has become common "entertainment." The movies leave little to the imagination and exhibit the most violent scenes of bondage, rape, and mutilation, the ultimate being the so-called "snuff" films where the victim is killed at the culmination of the abuser's sexual release.

Clearly, pornography today refers to the sexual stimulation of men by images that are abusive, degrading, or violent to

18

women. By this criterion, many of today's fashionable thrillers (**Dressed to Kill**) and horror movies are pornography.

Some scientists dealing with the study of aggression have stated that we women have "overinterpreted" the data. Yet a study in **Psychology Today** reports that many men watching a rape film saw the victim's pain as a sign of sexual excitement. And 51% of the men surveyed said that they would rape a woman if they could get away with it. In the 1970 report of the President's Commission on Pornography, 39% of all sex offenders said their crimes were influenced by pornography. . .

Soft-core pornography magazines are a cause of concern because of their socializing effect on the attitudes of the youth and men who read them. The circulation of **Playboy** and **Penthouse** is over four million copies each, and these magazines provide sex education for most American boys. Both these publications exploit women through pictures, cartoons, and articles that glorify violence and trivialize incest, child molestation, and rape.

Of course, as in most matters, the bottom line in the making and distribution of both hard- and soft-core pornography is profits. Recently, FBI director William H. Webster reported that pornography is a $4 billion-a-year industry (more than the combined profits of record and film industry) rooted deeply in organized crime. Thus, individual buyers support an industry that thrives and survives on the gross exploitation of women.

A Human Issue

Finally, it must be seen that the issue of rape and pornography is not just a woman's issue but a human issue. Women and children and men have been and are being raped and pornography is the most blatant exponent of rape. It is essential that all women and men realize that rape and violence are not normal forms of sexual excitement, and further that pornography is not "adult entertainment," but an abusive weapon that dehumanizes us all.

A CHRISTIAN PERSPECTIVE ON PORNOGRAPHY

American Lutheran Church

The following statement was adopted by the Seventeenth General Convention of the American Lutheran Church, as a statement of comment and counsel addressed to the members of the congregations of the American Lutheran Church to aid in their decisions and actions.

Points To Consider

1. What is the relationship between pornography and obscenity?
2. How can the evils of pornography be dealt with?
3. What did the Supreme Court say about "obscene materials?"

A statement of the American Lutheran Church adopted October 12, 1974.

Pornography is big business, supplying a product for which there is evident demand. Refusal to buy the product, and withholding patronage from those who offer the offending goods or services, strike at the profit core.

1. Pornography often is equated with obscenity. Pornography indeed may be obscene, but so are other matters not related to sex. Violence, war, double talk intended to deceive, exploiting or treating any other human being as a thing, engaging in manipulative selling, placing material interests ahead of human values—these too are obscene. Christians make a mistake when they leave the impression that it is only sex-oriented obscenities, not the whole range of offenses done to other human beings, which arouse their opposition.

2. Appeals to clamp down on pornography cause problems for Christians. They understand pornography to be material that depicts or describes erotic behavior in ways deliberately intended to stimulate sexual excitement. They regard human sexuality too highly to see it trifled with as a thing for the market place. Thus Christians easily respond to calls for sexual purity and morality in print, on the screen, and on the stage. However, deeper questions are involved in the usual efforts to curb pornography, such as:

—is it either right, necessary, or salutary to use civil laws to set standards for thoughts, tastes, and attitudes toward sexual practices?

—how can persons and communities be protected against sex-saturated materials and outlets which offend the sensitive or exploit the gullible?

—what room is there, with both freedom and responsibility, to explore issues and problems in human sexuality even though they run counter to current taboos and standards?

—why is so much of the sexual relegated to the realm of the forbidden and why is it made so difficult for people to appreciate their sexual selves and their sexual feelings?

—how does the Gospel liberate the believer from crippling enslavement both to prevailing sexual stereotypes and to self-centered pursuit of erotic pleasures?

3. Christians as citizens need to give thoughtful consideration to the issues involved in pornography. Two recent major events served to focus public attention on these issues. The first was the 1970 *Report of the Commission on Obscenity and Pornogra-*

phy, including the vigorous dissents registered by minority members. In summary, the Commission advocated "the right of adults who wish to do so to read, obtain, or view explicit sexual materials." It recommended legislation both to regulate "the sale of sexual materials to young persons who do not have the consent of their parents" and "to protect persons from having sexual materials thrust upon them without their consent through the mails or through open public display." Beyond the exceptions, the Commission recommended the repeal of all legislation prohibiting "the consensual sale, exhibition, or the distribution of sexual materials to adults."

DINNER IS SERVED

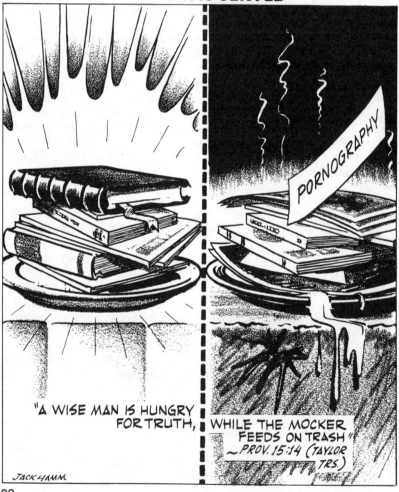

"A WISE MAN IS HUNGRY FOR TRUTH, WHILE THE MOCKER FEEDS ON TRASH"
~PROV. 15:14 (TAYLOR TRS.)

JACK HAMM

4. The second major event was the June 21, 1973 series of decisions by the Supreme Court of the United States reaffirming previous decisions that "obscene material is unprotected by the First Amendment." Acknowledging "the inherent dangers of undertaking to regulate any form of expression" the majority of the Court agreed to "confine the permissible scope of such regulations to works which depict or describe sexual conduct." The Court set three guidelines: "(a) whether the average person, applying contemporary community standards, would find that the work, taken as a whole, appeals to the prurient interest. . . . (b) whether the work depicts or describes, in a patently offensive way, sexual conduct specifically defined by the applicable state law, and (c) whether the work, taken as a whole, lacks serious literary, artistic, political, or scientific value." Far from settling the situation, the Court decisions raised further critical issues yet to be resolved.

5. Persons seriously interested in attacking the evils associated with pornography wisely would consider such points as the following:

a. Pornography is big business, supplying a product for which there is evident demand. Refusal to buy the product, and withholding patronage from those who offer the offending goods or services, strike at the profit core.

b. By most standards pornography is a low-grade, low quality, overpriced product that prostitutes the sexual side of human life. Good judgment and good taste argue against spending good money for inferior, shabby, degrading products.

c. Pornography preys on sexual ignorance, fears, and frustrations. Positive acceptance of oneself as a sexual being, and

---

Purposes of Sex

Our Creator designed sex in marriage for bringing happy children into the family and to bind husband and wife together in a sacred, giving relationship not shared with others. Both purposes are impossible with pornography.

British author J. B. Priestley put it this way: "Eroticism in itself, wanting a sensation and not another person, makes love impossible."

Jeff E. Zhorne, "The Polluting of Human Sexuality," *The Plain Truth,* February 1983.

healthy attitudes and orientation to human sexuality, reduce the lures of pornography.

d. The influence and example of parents and other trusted adults in their reading, viewing, leisure-time, and entertainment habits communicate powerfully to children and youth. Parental guidance, to be effective, needs reliable information concerning issues, materials, and curiosities currently in tension.

e. The law, the police, and the courts are the legal resources available for combating pornography. Cooperation between citizens and personnel in law enforcement systems is essential if a specific alleged violation is to be given its due judicial decision.

6. The church has the opportunity through the Spirit of God for creating new human beings who are free and responsible to live and act because of the power of the Gospel. The church teaches, on the basis of the whole of God's counsel, the importance of controls arising from within because of a person's relationship with the Living Lord. It stresses a person's right to make free choices, under God, accountable to God, considerate of the neighbor. Such choices take civil law into account, but take even more seriously God's Law and the Gospel revealed in His Son. Human freedom of course carries the risk that some persons will misuse their freedom. Human freedom also insures opportunity for many persons to grow in wisdom, knowledge, and favor with God and neighbor. Such freedom, applied to pornography, carries risks of misuse and exploitation. Such freedom, applied to pornography, also insures opportunity for many persons to grow in understanding and appreciation for God's gift of human sexuality.

7. For civil legislators the difficult task is (a) to balance freedom and responsibility, (b) to protect the sensitive and the gullible, (c) to assure a climate for open and honest discussion of issues related to human sexuality, (d) to define clearly that which is a scandal and an offense to standards of morality and integrity, and (e) to provide channels for adjudicating between competing sets of standards and values. How to achieve these goals is a perplexing exercise in political realities. Christian citizens will offer their counsel, their prayers, their support for what is good and wholesome, and their energies to correct what is evil and destructive in public policies dealing with pornography.

VALUES IN CONFLICT

A SOCIALIST PERSPECTIVE ON PORNOGRAPHY
Maggie McCraw

The author is a member of the Socialist Workers Party. She wrote this article for **The Militant,** *the national publication of the Socialist Workers Party. In her following comments she asserts that pornography is a symptom of capitalism and the economics of greed.*

Points to Consider

1. What is wrong with the censorship of pornography?
2. What is behind the production and distribution of pornography?
3. How can pornography and other social ills of our society be dealt with?

Maggie McCraw, "Debate Over Pornograpny," *The Militant,* March 23, 1984, pp. 23, 24.

Sexism and women's social powerlessness—
rooted in their economic dependence—cause
violence against women in a society where
violence and alienation are integral aspects of
social relations."

The Twin Cities Militant Forum sponsored a presentation by Andrea Morell, a longtime activist in the women's liberation movement and a member of the Socialist Workers Party National Committee. The title of her talk was: "Pornography: Where It Comes From, How It Can Be Abolished—A Marxist View. . . ."

Pornography is big business

Morell explained that pornography is big business—an estimated $7 billion a year in the United States. "One thing we do know pornography causes is *rich people*," she said. It is part of organized crime, which in turn is tied in with big business circles and protected by the government. Pornographers are "business associates" of pimps, drug pushers, gambling kings—the whole class of criminals which reaps enormous profit from workers' misery.

Morell took up the degradation and brutality pornographers visit on the female and child victims who are forced to make the films, photos, etc. Many of the women victims are drawn from the ranks of the unemployed, and many are undocumented workers who have no legal recourse against what happens to them.

Morell said that pornography is the polar opposite of the central idea of feminism—that women are human beings, not sex objects. "Pornography is reactionary. It glorifies the degrading social role which women are now in revolt *against*."

She also exposed the liberal myth that pornography is some form of "sexual liberation." "Feminists challenged this myth by pointing to the *real* message of pornography—that women are sexual slaves of men and love it. Pornography is not about female sexuality but about male sexual domination and brutalization of women—and the degradation of *all* human sexuality. It is not new or revolutionary; it is the basest sexual stereotype of women historically."

Morell pointed out that Black women have played an important role in exposing pornography's racist side. "Scenes of Black women in bondage are nothing but a glorification of the enslavement and degradation of Blacks under a sexual veneer. The

26

Playboy Awards

To show the contradiction in *Playboy*'s giving awards for freedom, the protesters presented Hefner "awards" of their own. Seven "Hugh M. Hefner Woman-Hating Awards" were given to *Playboy* for:

- *reducing women to bunnies, pets, and playthings;*
- *encouraging the harassment of women workers;*
- *portraying women of color in a racist manner;*
- *exploiting lesbianism;*
- *sexualizing little girls and joking about child abuse;*
- *ridiculing older women;*
- *promoting rape and violence against women.*

Women Against Pornography Newsreport, Fall/Winter 1983.

dangerous myth of the Black male rapist gets a big boost in pornography as well."

She also explained that child pornography is part of the sexual abuse of children in this society, 99 percent of whose victims are female.

Pornography and antiwoman violence

One of the main assertions made by supporters of the Minneapolis ordinance is that pornography causes rape, wife beating, and child abuse.

Morell responded, "There is a link, of course. But pornography is not *the cause* of these things. Antiwoman violence is caused by the entire unequal relationship between the sexes, with women the inferior sex, in this class-divided society. Sexism and women's social powerlessness—rooted in their economic dependence—cause violence against women in a society where violence and alienation are integral aspects of social relations."

What is pornography's role? "It is a particularly vicious part of the reactionary sexist ideology that permeates all of class society," said Morell. "It fosters an image of women as less than human."

Is pornography actual violence against women, as some who want the government to ban it contend? "We cannot make an identity between deeds and words," said Morell. "Pornography is not the same as actually being assaulted. Looking at pictures of a rape and actually committing a rape are two very different things. They are connected but hardly identical. Pornography is part of the reactionary ideological pressures bearing down on us—and should be confronted accordingly. It is an image and an idea that is harmful and should be struggled against and stamped out. Censorship laws, however, won't accomplish that."

Morell contrasted the attitude toward women held by the U.S. employers and their government with the policies of revolutionary governments in countries run by the workers and farmers.

"Today in Nicaragua, the Sandinista-led workers and farmers government promotes and defends the needs and interests of women. As part of this, not only is pornography illegal, but the exploitation of women's bodies in commercial advertising is illegal as well.

"But in Nicaragua, these laws are aimed against those who seek to profit from women's subordination. They don't result in censorship of the women's organization's magazine or the trade unions' newspapers. That's because the Nicaraguan government is on the side of the oppressed and exploited," said Morell.

Morell quoted from an article in *Plexus*, a San Francisco feminist paper. The article was written by two women who had visited revolutionary Grenada before the U.S. invasion. As one of the women said, "For the first time in my life I felt no fear. I felt

Nicaraguan women in reserve battalion. Pornography and sexist advertising have been outlawed in Nicaragua by revolutionary government that takes side of women against those who profit from their oppression.

free. . . . Women were really strong. Pornography was illegal. Women were not afraid to be on the street at night." They recalled that a popular slogan on billboards was, "Men stand firm, women step forward."

These policies of the People's Revolutionary Government led by slain Prime Minister Maurice Bishop are clearly the opposite of what the U.S. government promotes both at home and in its continued occupation of Grenada. . . .

Battle for public opinion

Morell encouraged feminists and their supporters to safeguard democratic rights. "Our battle right now is for public opinion. We need to explain why pornography is reactionary. Instead of promoting censorship, we should exercise our right to free speech by educating about pornography and the goals of women's liberation.

"This is one aspect of our fight for liberation. We also need to participate in the broader fight for abortion rights, affirmative action, child care, and the Equal Rights Amendment. We must seek allies, and take up issues such as war, racism, and union-busting as the feminist issues they are."

It will take decisive political action by the working class and its allies—especially the organized women's rights movement—to deal with the pornographers, Morell emphasized. The Democrats and Republicans won't do the job because they are the political servants of the wealthy ruling families.

Women's rights fighters need to turn their backs on these two parties and join with their allies in striking out on an independent political course.

"We need a labor party based on a fighting trade union movement, and an independent Black party," said Morell. "These will be women's rights parties, and will take on the criminal pornographers and their cohorts." This is a necessary part of the challenge to the current social order, which must include uprooting the parasites that live at the expense of workers and the oppressed.

Morell pointed out that rooting out the pornographers, as well as pimps and drug pushers, has been a part of all the socialist revolutions that have occurred. Anyone who has seen the movie *Godfather II* remembers the vivid images of this criminal element fleeing Cuba when the revolution triumphed there.

To accomplish the same goals in the United States, she said, "we need our own government, one that can organize to smash those who profit from pornography, women's oppression, racism, and class exploitation, and can lead society toward socialism, the only system that can create new men and new women."

29

WHAT IS EDITORIAL BIAS?

This activity may be used as an individualized study guide for students in libraries and resource centers or as a discussion catalyst in small group and classroom discussions.

The capacity to recognize an author's point of view is an essential reading skill. The skill to read with insight and understanding involves the ability to detect different kinds of opinions or bias. Sex bias, race bias, ethnocentric bias, political bias and religious bias are five basic kinds of opinions expressed in editorials and all literature that attempts to persuade. They are briefly defined in the glossary below.

GLOSSARY OF TERMS FOR READING SKILLS

sex bias—the expression of dislike for and/or feeling of superiority over the opposite sex or a particular sexual minority

race bias—the expression of dislike for and/or feeling of superiority over a racial group

ethnocentric bias—the expression of a belief that one's own group, race, religion, culture or nation is superior. Ethnocentric persons judge others by their own standards and values.

political bias—the expression of political opinions and attitudes about domestic or foreign affairs

religious bias—the expression of a religious belief or attitude

Guidelines

1. From the readings in chapter one, locate five sentences that provide examples of editorial opinion or bias.

2. Write down each of the above sentences and determine what kind of bias each sentence represents. Is it sex bias, race bias, ethnocentric bias, political bias or religious bias?

3. Make up one sentence statements that would be an example of each of the following: *sex bias, race bias, ethnocentric bias, political bias* and *religious bias.*

4. See if you can locate five sentences that are factual statements from the readings in chapter one.

5. What is the editorial message of the cartoon in reading number three?

CHAPTER 2

DOES PORNOGRAPHY CAUSE VIOLENCE?
Points and Counterpoints

CHAPTER OVERVIEW

DOES PORNOGRAPHY CAUSE VIOLENCE?
Debating the Issue

Chapter Overview

Since the publication of the **President's Commission on Obscenity and Pornography** in 1970, a national debate has continued about the effects of sexually explicit materials. Many social scientists feel the commission report has generally settled the issue. The commission found that pornography does not have any demonstrable adverse effects. The commission study by Berl Kutchinsky even found some positive results using statistics he claimed showed a drop in sex crimes in Denmark following the release of all censorship in that country.

The commission's findings, however, have not silenced the debate. Many feminists, political groups, investigators, and scientists have been critical, and believe pornography contributes to violence against women. Edward Donnerstein and Neil Malamuth have been leaders in research on the effects of aggressive pornography. These researchers say that aggressive pornographic materials were relatively infrequent at the time of the commission study in 1970. They claim the increase in availability of aggressive pornography may have adverse social outcomes because "research findings indicate that aggressive pornography affects aggression against women within the laboratory." Feminists like Andrea Dworkin and Catherine Mackinnon define pornography as the "celebration, promotion, and legitimization of rape and violence against women. They view it as the sexuality of male supremacy and a violation of women's civil rights. Efforts have been made in major cities to legally ban pornography on the basis that it is a form of discrimination. The readings in this chapter present conflicting interpretations about the social implications of pornography, especially its effect on women.

LINKING PORNOGRAPHY TO SEX CRIMES

The Commission on Obscenity and Pornography

Congress, in Public Law 90–100, found the traffic in obscenity and pornography to be "a matter of national concern." The Federal Government was deemed to have a "responsibility to investigate the gravity of this situation and to determine whether such materials are harmful to the public, and particularly to minors, and whether more effective methods should be devised to control the transmission of such materials. To this end, the Congress established an advisory commission. The commission report still has many supporters today and is a great source of controversy now, as it was at the time of publication in 1970. The following excerpts from the report summarize the basic conclusions of the study.

Points To Consider

1. How is the purpose of the Commission described?
2. What was the major finding about the relationship between pornography and sexual violence?

Excerpted from **The Report of the Commission On Obscenity and Pornography,** September, 1970.

Empirical research designed to clarify the question has found no evidence to date that exposure to explicit sexual materials plays a significant role in the causation of delinquent or criminal behavior among youth or adults.

There is no consensus among Americans regarding what they consider to be the effects of viewing or reading explicit sexual materials. A diverse and perhaps inconsistent set of beliefs concerning the effects of sexual materials is held by large and necessarily overlapping portions of American men and women. Between 40% and 60% believe that sexual materials provide information about sex, provide entertainment, lead to moral breakdown, improve sexual relationships of married couples, lead people to commit rape, produce boredom with sexual materials, encourage innovation in marital sexual technique and lead people to lose respect for women. Some of these presumed effects are obviously socially undesirable while others may be regarded as socially neutral or desirable. When questioned about effects, persons were more likely to report having personally experienced desirable than undesirable ones. Among those who believed undesirable effects had occurred, there was a greater likelihood of attributing their occurrences to others than to self. But mostly, the undesirable effects were just believed to have happened without reference to self or personal acquaintances.

Surveys of psychiatrists, psychologists, sex educators, social workers, counselors and similar professional workers reveal that large majorities of such groups believe that sexual materials do not have harmful effects on either adults or adolescents. On the other hand, a survey of police chiefs found that 58% believed that "obscene" books played a significant role in causing juvenile delinquency. . .

Criminal And Delinquent Behavior

Delinquent and nondelinquent youth report generally similar experiences with explicit sexual materials. Exposure to sexual materials is widespread among both groups. The age of first exposure, the kinds of materials to which they are exposed, the amount of their exposure, the circumstances of exposure, and their reactions to erotic stimuli are essentially the same, particularly when family and neighborhood backgrounds are held constant. There is some evidence that peer group pressure accounts for both sexual experience and exposure to erotic materials

35

among youth. A study of a heterogeneous group of young people found that exposure to erotica had no impact upon moral character over and above that of a generally deviant background.

Statistical studies of the relationship between availability of erotic materials and the rates of sex crimes in Denmark indicate that the increased availability of explicit sexual materials has been accompanied by a decrease in the incidence of sexual crime. Analysis of police records of the same types of sex crimes in Copenhagen during the past 12 years revealed that a dramatic decrease in reported sex crimes occurred during this period and that the decrease coincided with changes in Danish law which permitted wider availability of explicit sexual materials. Other research showed that the decrease in reported sexual offenses cannot be attributed to concurrent changes in the social and legal definitions of sex crimes or in public attitudes toward reporting such crimes to the police, or in police reporting procedures.

The United States

Statistical studies of the relationship between the availability of erotic material and the rates of sex crimes in the United States presents a more complex picture. During the period in which there has been a marked increase in the availability of erotic materials, some specific rates of arrest for sex crimes have increased (*e.g.*, forcible rape) and others have declined (*e.g.*, overall juvenile rates). For juveniles, the overall rate of arrests for sex crimes decreased even though arrests for nonsexual crimes increased by more than 100%. For adults, arrests for sex offenses increased slightly more than did arrests for nonsex offenses. The conclusion is that, for America, the relationship between the availability of erotica and changes in sex crime rates neither proves nor disproves the possibility that availability of erotica leads to crime, but the massive overall increases in sex crimes that have been alleged do not seem to have occurred.

Available research indicates that sex offenders have had less adolescent experience with erotica than other adults. They do not differ significantly from other adults in relation to adult experience with erotica, in relation to reported arousal or in relation to the likelihood of engaging in sexual behavior during or following exposure. Available evidence suggests that sex offenders' early inexperience with erotic material is a reflection of their more generally deprived sexual environment. The relative absence of experience appears to constitute another indicator of atypical and inadequate sexual socialization.

In sum, empirical research designed to clarify the question has found no evidence to date that exposure to explicit sexual materials plays a significant role in the causation of delinquent or criminal behavior among youth or adults. The Commission cannot conclude that exposure to erotic materials is a factor in the causation of sex crime or sex delinquency.

Pornography And Crime

Besides being basically harmless, pornography may indeed have positive benefits as an instrument of crime control. Unfortunately, the lack of academic respectability attached to the subject has tended to block empirical investigation of this possibility . . .

Controlled exposure to pornography is certainly useful in sex education and treatment programs . . .

Beryl Kutchinsky, *Encyclopedia of Crime And Justice*, MacMillan, 1983.

LINKING PORNOGRAPHY TO SEX CRIMES

Catherine A. Mackinnon

*Catherine Mackinnon is an attorney and associate
professor at the University of Minnesota Law School. She
and Andrea Dworkin drafted the Minneapolis
Antipornography Ordinance. It was an attempt to ban
pornography as a form of sexual discrimination against
women.*

Points To Consider

1. How is pornography defined?
2. Who is harmed by pornography?

Catherine A. Mackinnon, "Pornography: A Feminist Perspective," position paper for the Minneapolis City Council, December, 1983.

Simply put, pornography eroticizes dominance and submission, of which rape, battery, sexual harassment, and the sexual and physical abuse of children are also forms of practice.

I want to talk about pornography from the feminist view. Pornography is the celebration, the promotion, the authorization and the legitimization of rape, sexual harassment, battery and the abuse of children. All for the purpose of the sexual pleasure of men. Simply put pornography eroticizes dominance and submission, of which rape, battery, sexual harassment, and the sexual and physical abuse of children are also forms of practice. It is affirmatively employing the enforcement of others' powerlessness. In this perspective, pornography is not, as it is often considered, an insanity or a deviation. Given the pervasiveness of the abuses I have characterized, it can not be seen as a corrupt and confused misrepresentation of what is otherwise a natural, healthy sexual situation. It is not a distortion, a reflection, a projection, an expression, or a symbol either. It is the sexuality of male supremacy. . .

The View of Pornography

In the view of pornography women desire dispossession and cruelty. We **want** to be battered and raped and sexually harassed. In pornography we have men permitted to create scenarios in which we can be whoever they want. What do they want? (A question they usually ask about us.) Permitted to put words as well as many other things into women's mouths, they create scenes in which women desperately want to be bound, battered, tortured, raped, humiliated and killed. We want it, we beg for it, we get it. I have to conclude that this is erotic to the male standpoint. I learn from pornography that subjection itself, specifically the ecstatic relinquishment of one's self-determination, is the content of women's sexual desirability. It is also presented as the content of our sexual desire. We are in pornography to be violated. Men are there to violate us, on-screen, by camera, by the pen and on behalf of the viewers. Is this equality?

Pornography is often defended as a beginning of the equality of human sexual liberation. This defense, by lawyers or neo-Freudians, or feminists, is that pornography is there to help free women. From the feminist perspective I have sketched, it is a defense not only of force, of the sexual terrorism of rape, but of the subordination of women to men clear and simple. In this sense, sexual liberation means freeing male sexual aggression. What in the defense of pornography is called love and romance, in the feminist viewpoint is hatred. What in the defense of pornography is called pleasure and eroticism, in the feminist perspective is violation. What they call desire, we call lust for dominance and submission.

Pornography And Violence

The first thing to be observed about pornography as a genre is that it is premised upon the actual physical practice of rape, torture and humiliation. Those pictures you see are being done to someone. The men who wrote those books did, and do, what they write about, on some level. That person you have depicted, that being, is a real live woman. The free speech of the pornographers, before it was their speech, was someone's life. A specific **person's** life. . .

There are studies showing increasingly firm connections between exposure to pornography and increases in abusive attitudes and behaviors toward women. . . Go to the corner of Central and Fourth to an emporium of pornography I believe is owned by the Alexander brothers. The definition of women as a group that enjoys pain, enjoys rape, can't wait to be tied up, is

Reprinted with permission from the Minneapolis Star and Tribune.

Pornography In Denmark

Since Denmark lifted its censorship laws on pornography a decade ago, it has been referred to repeatedly as proof that sexual offenses decrease when pornography is allowed to flourish. In 1970, for example, the Commission on Obscenity and Pornography cited two Danish studies which claimed that sex crimes were down in Denmark as a result of liberalized pornography laws. The commission used those studies to bolster its own finding—that pornography was "harmless." But recent research shows these studies were incomplete, inadequate, and biased on several counts.

It is also important to note, as Jean-Claude Lauret points out, that pro-pornography arguments from Denmark are suspect: Pornography is the third largest industry (after agriculture and furniture-making) in Denmark, bringing in $60 million per year. This is a strong incentive to the government to keep stories and statistics of rape and violence under cover.

Diana E. H. Russel, "Testimony Against Pornography," *Take Back The Night,* Ed. by Lederer and Rich, Bantam Books, 1982.

dying to be sexually harassed, is what I am confident you will see there. That is why women mostly avoid pornography. . .

So long as pornography exists, there will be no equality, and the idea that we live in an equal society will be a vicious illusion.

PORNOGRAPHY CAN REDUCE SEX CRIMES

Berl Kutchinsky

Berl Kutchinsky is a social scientist and researcher associated with the Institute of Criminal Science at the University of Copenhagen. The following statement is excerpted from his controversial study explaining the decrease in registered sex crimes in Copenhagen.

Points To Consider

1. What sex crimes decreased in Copenhagen?
2. What is the "safety valve theory?"
3. What is the major conclusion of Kutchinsky's study?

Berl Kutchinsky, The Report of the Commission on Obscenity and Pornography, 1970, Vol. VII.

It seems likely that some earlier offenders may have stopped or at least reduced their criminal activity, while potential new offenders may never engage in committing sexual offenses because they get sufficient sexual satisfaction through the use of pornography.

Recent years have seen a dramatic decrease in the number of sexual offenses registered by the police in Copenhagen. The decrease has taken place in practically all areas of sex crimes, although there are certain variations. Thus, the largest drop was seen with peeping, exhibitionism, and indecent interference with girls, while there was only a small decrease in rape or attempted rape.

While the number of sex crimes had been rather stable for many years, a downward trend became manifest in the first part of the 1960's, and from the middle of the decade the decrease became striking. Table 1 presents an excerpt of the police statistics, giving an impression of the change that has taken place. . .

Table 1

SURVEY ON SEX CRIMES: SEXUAL OFFENSES AGAINST FEMALES
(Excerpts from police statistics for Copenhagen)

	1959	1964	1969	1959–1969 Relative decrease	Total no. of cases 1958-1969	
Type of sex crime:	No.	No.	No.	%	No.	%
Rape	32	20	27	—	309	3.7
Exhibitionism	249	225	104	58.2	2617	31.6
Peeping	99	61	20	79.8	742	9.0
Coitus with minors	51	18	19	62.7	380	4.6
Verbal indecency	45	43	13	71.1	467	5.6
Other indecency (women)	137	103	60	56.2	1353	16.3
Other indecency (girls)	282	204	87	69.1	2416	29.2
Total	895	674	330		8284	100.0

43

Many theories have been put forward concerning the relationship between pornography and sex crimes. We will not engage in that discussion but merely consider the one theory which is applicable in the present context, the so-called "safety valve" theory. For our purpose, we restate this theory in the following way: It is unquestionable that with few exceptions the purpose of the sexual offender when committing a sex crime is to obtain sexual satisfaction, usually in the form of orgasm. In many cases of sex crimes, the orgasm is obtained through masturbation either while committing the crime or immediately afterwards. Since pornography is well suited (and quite often used) as a source of sexual stimulation for masturbation, it seems likely that some earlier offenders may have stopped or at least reduced their criminal activity, while potential new offenders may never engage in committing sexual offenses because they get sufficient sexual satisfaction through the use of pornography. (Hereafter we refer to this possible explanation of the decrease in registered sex crimes in Copenhagen as the "pornography factor" theory.)

An apparent objection to this theory is that, according to the findings of Gebhard, Gagnon, Pomeroy, and Christenson (1965, p. 669ff.) sexual offenders are not, as a rule, more sexually

Pornography And Rape

One looks in vain even for documentation that growth in exposure to aggressive pornography was indeed accompanied or followed by an equal growth in the incidence of forcible-rape—although even to establish such a temporal link would not prove causality . . .

Rape statistics in countries where pornography—especially aggressive pornography—is easily obtainable produce results even more devastating to claimed links between pornography and rape. In West Germany the rape rates remained remarkably steady, in fact with a slight decrease, amounting to 6 percent, between 1972 and 1979—and in 1973 most forms of pornography were legalized, with aggressive pornography (still illegal) being easily accessible.

Beryl Kutchinsky, *Encyclopedia of Crime and Justice*: MacMillan, 1983.

aroused by pornography than noncriminal males—in fact, some types of sexual offenders seem to be much less responsive to pornography than are other men. One reason for this would be, according to the same authors, that the use of pornography requires the ability to empathize and fantasize, an ability which is correlated with education. The poorly educated, a group to which the majority of sexual offenders belong, "are apt to be much more pragmatic and require something more concrete in order to respond" (Gebhard et al., 1965, p. 671).

This objection seems relevant to the "pornography factor" theory of the decrease, as concerns the effect of the "porno' literature wave." The abundance of pornographic books could be expected to be used as a "safety valve" only by the better educated (or more intelligent) potential sex offenders. The picture pornography, on the other hand, is not affected by this objection: on the contrary, one might expect that these "full color" magazines and films with the reputation of "leaving nothing to fantasy" would be very well suited as a means of sexual stimulation for persons with a poor imagination, who need "something more concrete". . .

Conclusion

We have completed an analysis in which we have tried to combine information from several different sources, including the tentative findings in the present survey, in order to explain the recent decrease in the numbers of four different types of sex crimes registered by the police in Copenhagen. Concerning three of these types of crimes—exhibitionism, peeping, and (physical) indecency towards girls—it was possible, without restraint or ad hoc constructions, tentatively to explain this registered decrease as being due to the influence on either the victims or the potential offenders of one single factor, namely the development in the availability of pornography. While the general change in the sexual behavior and attitudes of the Danes may, in different ways, have had a contributory influence on the decrease of the above three types of sex crimes, the analysis tentatively indicated that the influence of such a change on the *victims* was the major reason for the registered decrease in (physical) indecency towards women.

For two types of sex crimes—peeping and (physical) indecency towards girls—the analysis led to the tentative conclusion that the abundant availability of hard-core pornography in Denmark may have been the direct cause of a veritable decrease in the actual amount of crime committed.

It is realized that the perspectives of these conclusions—if they are true—are considerable. We should therefore like to stress once more that the conclusions are tentative and will have to be reexamined on the basis of a more complete analysis of this survey and the crime statistics. Others will have to judge whether these preliminary conclusions carry enough weight to have any political consequences. There is no doubt, however, that they should result in a serious effort to examine the theory that pornography may prevent certain types of sex crimes, especially sexual offenses against children.

PORNOGRAPHY MAY LEAD TO SEXUAL VIOLENCE
Edward Donnerstein and Daniel Linz

Edward Donnerstein is a psychologist in the Center for Communication Research at the communication arts department of the University of Wisconsin. Daniel Linz is in the psychology department at the University of Wisconsin.

Points To Consider

1. What do the authors say about the President's Commission on Obscenity and Violence?
2. What new factors lead some social scientists to think that pornography might lead to sexual violence?
3. What conclusions have the authors reached from their studies?

Researchers have shown, for example, that exposure to even a few minutes of sexually violent pornography, such as scenes of rape and other forms of sexual violence against women, can lead to antisocial attitudes and behavior.

The President's Commission on Obscenity and Pornography concluded in 1970 that there was no relationship between exposure to erotic material and subsequent antisocial behavior. Many liberals and people opposed to censorship of any kind applauded this finding, but some social scientists were more cautious and warned that pornography, especially violent pornography, might heighten the chances that some viewers would behave in bizarre or antisocial ways. In light of the increasingly violent nature of pornography and the results of ongoing research that focuses on the fusion of sex and violence, those warnings probably should be taken seriously.

Researchers have shown, for example, that exposure to even a few minutes of sexually violent pornography, such as scenes of rape and other forms of sexual violence against women, can lead to antisocial attitudes and behavior: It can increase the viewer's acceptance of rape myths (for example, that women want to be raped), increase the willingness of a man to say that he would commit a rape, increase aggressive behavior against women in a laboratory setting and decrease one's sensitivity to rape and the plight of the rape victim. If a brief exposure to sexually violent pornography can have these effects, what are the effects of exposure to hours of such material?

Habituation

As depictions of sex and violence become more numerous and increasingly graphic, especially in feature-length movies shown in theaters, officials at the National Institute of Mental Health are becoming concerned and note:

"Films had to be made more and more powerful in their arousal effects. Initially strong excitatory reactions (may grow) weak or vanish entirely with repeated exposure to stimuli of a certain kind. This is known as habituation. The possibility of habituation to sex and violence has significant social consequences. . . .If people become inured to violence from seeing much of it, they may be less likely to respond to real violence."

This loss of sensitivity to real violence after repeated exposure to films with sex and violence, or "the dilemma of the detached

Employee at the Eighth Street Playhouse, New York City

bystander in the presence of violence'' (a topic to which social scientists should be directing more of their efforts, according to the Surgeon General, C. Everett Koop), is the major focus of our research program at the University of Wisconsin in Madison. We and our colleague, Stephen Penrod, are investigating how massive exposure to commercially released sexually violent films influences viewer perceptions of violence, judgments about rape and rape victims and general physiological desensitization to violence and aggressive behavior.

Unlike previous studies in which subjects may have seen only 10 to 30 minutes of material, the current studies eventually will examine up to 25 hours of exposure and allow us to monitor the process of desensitization in subjects over a long period of time. We will examine not only aggressive behavior, but perceptual and judgmental changes regarding violence, and we will look for ways of mitigating potential negative aftereffects of exposure to mass-media violence.

Filmed Violence

We already have conducted a study to monitor desensitization of males to filmed violence against women and to determine whether this desensitization "spilled over" into other decision-making about victims. Male subjects watched nearly 10 hours (five commercially released feature-length films, one a day for five days) of R-rated or X-rated movies. They saw either R-rated, sexually violent films such as *Tool Box Murders, Vice Squad, I Spit On Your Grave* and *Texas Chainsaw Massacre;* X-rated movies that depicted sexual assault; or X-rated movies that showed only consenting sex. The R-rated films were much more explicit with regard to violence than they were with regard to sexual content. After each movie, the men completed a mood questionnaire and evaluated the films in several ways. The films were shown in reverse order to different groups of men so that comparisons could be made of the same films being shown on the first and last day of viewing.

After the week of viewing, the men watched yet another film. This time, however, they saw a reenactment of an actual rape trial. After the trial, they were asked to render judgments about how responsible the victim was for her rape and how much injury she had suffered.

Most interesting were the results from the men who had watched the R-rated films such as *Texas Chainsaw Massacre* or *Maniac.* After the first day of viewing, the men rated themselves as significantly above the norm for depression, anxiety and annoyance. On each subsequent day of viewing, these scores dropped until, on the fourth day of viewing, their reported levels were back to normal. What had happened to the viewers as they watched more and more violence?

Our Conclusions

We argue that they were becoming desensitized to violence, particularly against women. But this entailed more than a simple lowering of arousal to the movie violence. The men began to actually perceive the films differently as time went on. On Day 1, for example, on the average, the men estimated that they had seen four "offensive scenes." By the fifth day, they reported only half as many offensive scenes (even though exactly the same movies, but in reverse order, had been shown). Likewise, their ratings of the violence within the films receded from Day 1 to Day 5. By the last day, the men rated the movies as less graphic and less gory and estimated a fewer number of violent scenes than on the first day of viewing. Most startling, by the last day of viewing graphic violence against women, the men were rating

50

the material as significantly less debasing and degrading to women, more humorous and more enjoyable, and they claimed a greater willingness to see this type of film again. This change in perception due to repeated exposure was particularly evident in comparisons of reactions to two films, *I Spit On Your Grave* and *Vice Squad.* Both films contain sexual assault; however, rape is portrayed in a more graphic and detailed manner in *I Spit On Your Grave* and a more ambiguous manner in *Vice Squad.* For men who had been exposed first to *Vice Squad* and then to *I Spit On Your Grave,* the ratings of sexual violence were nearly identical. However, subjects who had seen the more graphic movie first saw much less sexual violence (rape) in the more ambiguous film.

The effects of desensitization were also evident in the subjects' reactions to the re-enacted rape trial. The victim of rape was rated as significantly more worthless and her injury as significantly less severe by those men who had been exposed to filmed violence than by a control group who saw only the rape trial and did not view any of our films.

Where does the research go from here? We will continue to investigate desensitization effects in reported mood and anxiety ratings, as well as physiologically. Massive exposure to films portraying violence against women will be used to study aggression against women (in a laboratory setting). And we will look into the effects of movies that do not explicitly portray violence against women but that perpetuate ideas about women as sexual objects (the new wave of teenage sex films such as *Porky's* and *My Tutor.*

Finally, we are searching for ways to counter the negative effects we have been finding. The subjects in all of our studies receive extensive debriefing after seeing the film. These debriefings take the form of sessions with the experimenters and videotaped presentations that dispel certain myths about rape and attempt to "resensitize" subjects to the issue of violence, particularly violence against women. We have found that these debriefings produce a marked decrease in acceptance of rape myths and violence against women. We are also investigating the effects these debriefings have when presented to subjects prior to viewing the films. If this proves to be effective, it might eventually be advisable to package sexually violent films with a warning that would help counter the negative effects of exposure to mass-media sexual violence.

WHAT IS SEX BIAS?

This activity may be used as an individual study guide for students in libraries and resource centers or as a discussion catalyst in small group and classroom discussions.

Many readers are unaware that written material usually expresses an opinion or bias. The skill to read with insight and understanding requires the ability to detect different kinds of bias. Political bias, race bias, sex bias, ethnocentric bias and religious bias are five basic kinds of opinions expressed in editorials and literature that attempt to persuade. This activity will focus on sex bias defined in the glossary below.

5 KINDS OF EDITORIAL OPINION OR BIAS

sex bias—the expression of dislike for and/or feeling of superiority over a person because of gender or sexual preference

race bias—the expression of dislike for and/or feeling of superiority over a racial group

ethnocentric bias—the expression of a belief that one's own group, race, religion, culture or nation is superior. Ethnocentric persons judge others by their own standards and values.

political bias—the expression of opinions and attitudes about government-related issues on the local, state, national or international level

religious bias—the expression of a religious belief or attitude

Guidelines

Read through the following statements and decide which ones represent sex opinion or bias. Evaluate each statement by using the method indicated below.

Mark (S) for statements that reflect any sex bias.
Mark (O) for statements that reflect other kinds of opinion or bias.
Mark (F) for any factual statements.
Mark (N) for any statements that you are not sure about.

_____ 1. Pornography is often defended as a beginning of the equality of human sexual liberation.

_____ 2. Cities are examples of man-made environments that often conflict with and are hostile to the natural environment.

_____ 3. There are lots of studies that establish connections between the viewing of pornography and many forms of abusive attitudes and behavior towards women.

_____ 4. Men who enjoy pornography enjoy the degradation of women.

_____ 5. Pioneers trekked over the mountains with their wives, children, and cattle.

_____ 6. Movie viewers become desensitized to violence against women after repeated showings of the same film.

_____ 7. Since 1970 there has been a marked increase in the fusion of sex with violence in pornography.

_____ 8. The average citizen of any nation is proud of his heritage.

_____ 9. So long as pornography exists, there will be no equality, and the idea that we live in an equal society will be an illusion.

_____10. Men since the beginning of time have sought peace.

_____11. Research has found little evidence that exposure to pornographic materials is a factor in the cause of sex crimes or sex delinquency.

_____12. Common sense should tell us that exposure to explicit sexual materials will promote anti-social behavior, sex crimes, and sex delinquency.

_____13. Pornography is a lucrative business for many producers and distributors.

Other activities

1. Locate three examples of political opinion or bias in the readings from chapter two.
2. Make up one statement that would be an example of each of the following: *sex bias, race bias, ethnocentric bias,* and *religious bias.*

CHAPTER 3

PORNOGRAPHY, CENSORSHIP AND FREE SPEECH
Ideas in Conflict

BANNING PORNOGRAPHY AS DISCRIMINATION
Judith Pasternak

CHAPTER OVERVIEW

On April 23 Indianapolis became the second city in the nation to pass a controversial new type of antipornography ordinance, which defines pornography as an intrinsic violation of women's civil rights.

This view of pornography, plus the ordinance's underlying assumption that pornography is linked to violence against women, makes it new in the fight against pornography. At the same time, the ordinance has drawn fire from civil libertarians, who see its vagueness as harmful to free expression and possibly unconstitutional. And in Indianapolis, the bill was only passed through the alliance of an odd coalition of feminists and religious fundamentalists.

A similar antipornography bill was passed in Minneapolis last winter but later vetoed by the city's mayor, Don Fraser. Indianapolis Mayor William Hudnut, however, says he plans to sign his city's ordinance. But the Indiana Civil Liberties Union (ICLU), the American Civil Liberties Union and publishers, periodical distributors and the American Booksellers Association plan to challenge the bill's constitutionality.

The main premise of the ordinance is that pornography is "central in creating and maintaining sex as a basis for discrimination . . . [and] is a systematic practice of exploitation and subordination based on sex which differentially harms women."

The brainchild of University of Minnesota law professor Catherine McKinnon and antipornography activist and writer Andrea Dworkin, this type of ordinance originated in Minneapolis in 1983, when the city council there hired the two women to draft it as an amendment to the local civil rights ordinance.

By defining pornography itself as a violation of women's civil rights, the authors hoped to eliminate the need to prove in individual cases that any given piece of pornography actually harms

Excerpted from Judith Pasternak, "Feminists, Fundamentalists Get Antiporn Statute," **Guardian,** May 2, 1984.

55

anyone. Rather, if a particular item falls under the ordinance's definition of pornography, any person "injured" by it—and its mere presence constitutes an injury—can bring suit before a civil rights commission or court to have the item banned from sale within that jurisdiction.

Both the Indianapolis and Minneapolis ordinances provide new definitions of pornography. Both focus on the "sexually explicit subordination of women, graphically depicted," and the presentation of women as "sexual objects who enjoy pain and humiliation," "sexual objects who experience sexual pleasure in being raped," and "sexual objects tied up or cut up or mutilated." Many civil libertarians who oppose the ordinances consider these definitions vague enough to include literature and art never intended to be pornographic. Proponents claim, on the other hand, that the definitions are so specific as to render it almost impossible for nonexploitative works to be censored.

(Editor's Note: The readings in this chapter present Ideas In Conflict on the question of censoring pornography as a violation of women's civil rights.)

PORNOGRAPHY AND THE FIRST AMENDMENT

George Will

George Will is a nationally syndicated columnist. He is a leading spokesman in the print and electronic media for conservative ideas and causes. He makes regular appearances on the television shows that offer political commentary.

Points To Consider

1. What kind of pornography ordinance did the Minneapolis city council pass?
2. How does the author describe the inner life?
3. Why does he favor censorship of pornography?

The freedom of speech clause looks as though it has been trampled by a naked dancer, which in a sense it has. Various courts have decided that the clause was designed to protect not just speech—a capacity connected with reasoning and ideas, and hence self-government—but "expression," including that of naked dancers.

By the time peace spread her gentle wings over the Minneapolis City Council it had, by a 7-to-6 vote, done something innovative. In doing so it showed how awkward are attempts to act wisely on unwise premises.

The council came out for censorship, declaring pornography to be a form of illegal sex discrimination. Had the mayor not vetoed the measure, even the panorama of skin that assaults the senses of anyone approaching a normal newsstand would have violated the civil rights of all Minneapolis women, regardless of whether they are exposed to or affronted by it.

The amendment to the city's civil rights law would have defined pornography as the practice of "exploitation and subordination based on sex which differentially harms women." That is part of a remarkable statement of "findings":

"The bigotry and contempt (pornography) promotes, with the acts of aggression it fosters, harm women's opportunities for equality of rights in employment, education, property rights, public accommodations and public services; create public harassment and private denigration; promote injury and degradation such as rape, battery and prostitution and inhibit just enforcement of laws against these acts; contribute significantly to restricting women from full exercise of citizenship and participation in public life, including in neighborhoods; damage relations between the sexes; and undermine women's equal exercise of rights to speech and action . . ."

Although most of those assertions may be true, or true enough, it is hard to say how they constitute "findings." The assertions (here is another: "pornography is central in creating and maintaining the civil inequality of the sexes") are overreaching, a tactic of desperation. Why is such extravagance necessary? Because the logic of today's jurisprudence requires such unreasonableness before reasonable action can be taken.

58

"Hey, I know how we can shut them down. . . . Let's tell the Supreme Court the dancers always open their act with prayer!"

The Inner Life

It should not be necessary, before using law to sustain minimal decencies, to pretend that one can demonstrate that the polluting touch of pornography produces this or that particular behavior. But the Minneapolis law bristles with such assertions because today's judicial fashion holds that (in Felix Frankfurter's words) "law is concerned with external behavior and not the inner life of man."

It would be more sensible to say, as proper conservatives do: Behavior is a consequence of the inner life. Besides, the soul of the citizenry reveals the success of the country. We judge a nation by the character of its citizens, and common sense unassisted by sociological "findings" tells us that pornography is coarsening, and hence injurious to the community, and especially to women. Even more destructive than pornography are libertarian laws that express the doctrine that law should be indifferent to the evolution of the nation's character—to the inner life. So censorship of the most execrable material is wise.

Alas, the First Amendment as currently construed proscribes commonsense. The freedom of speech clause looks as though it has been trampled by a naked dancer, which in a sense it has. Various courts have decided that the clause was designed to protect not just speech—a capacity connected with reasoning and ideas, and hence self-government—but "expression," including that of naked dancers.

The mayor of Minneapolis said the measure went beyond the regulation of conduct to the impermissible regulation of "the transmission of ideas which may or may not have a causal relationship with illegal conduct." It is odd to speak of "ideas" being transmitted in pornographic movies, but that is not the only example here of the brittleness of the inapposite language of liberalism.

Severe Individualism

Proponents of the amendment, including some famous liberal feminists, obviously, and sensibly, considered it a measure to protect the moral tone of the community. Yet, they rattle on and on about individual rights and equality. Contemporary liberalism is a doctrine of such severe individualism that liberals, including the amendment's authors, can not use the vocabulary of collective concerns. They can not speak about the needs and rights of communities combatting a $7-billion industry in pornography.

A wise woman once wrote that sex is the Tabasco sauce that a nation with an adolescent palate sprinkles on every course in the menu. But the Supreme Court has left local authorities with some power over the crudest uses of the sauce. Local standards can be consulted when regulating material that appeals to prurient interests and is without literary, artistic, political or scientific value. If women can find more convincing language to use when pressing the point they made in Minneapolis, and I wish them well, they will alter community standards and thereby perhaps expand the power of local authorities to regulate pornography.

FIGHT PORN IN THE STREETS, NOT THE COURTS

Roanne Hindin

Roanne Hindin is an organizer of the San Francisco branch of Radical Women, the oldest socialist feminist national organization in the country. The following article appeared in **The Guardian**.

Points To Consider

1. Why is antipornography legislation a risky affair?
2. What is wrong with the Minneapolis antipornography sex discrimination amendment?
3. How can pornography be opposed most effectively?

Roanne Hindin, "Fight Porn in the Streets, Not the Courts," **The Guardian,** March 21, 1984, p. 7.

A primary shortcoming of the sex discrimination amendment is that it defines pornography as victimizing women exclusively.

Pornography, a $7 billion-a-year mob-dominated industry, is proliferating, scavenging off a decaying economic system which promotes child abuse for profit.

A woman stuffed head first into a meat grinder . . . a movie, "See exotic Oriental chicks loving to submit" . . . a movie called "Snuff" depicting the rape, murder and disembowelment of a woman.

Every day we are bombarded with these "natural" links between sex and violence, with the lie that women want and deserve to be humiliated and brutalized, that violence against women is normal, admirable and vital to male sexuality and privilege.

Feminists are leading the attack on this industry, denouncing porn as terrorism against women and children, as sexist and racist, and as degrading to women and men. With economic hard times at hand and the erosion of the gains of women and people of color, porn kings have intensified the sordidness of their product. Porn applies to the growing number of men already dehumanized by capitalism and deepens the divisions between men and women, and between races, through the use of stereotypes.

The porn industry leads the assault. The mainstream media and advertising follow with their own slightly watered-down images of anti-female violence.

Porn films have long since moved on to their logical extreme with "kiddie porn"—the sexual use of children—and "snuff" films. To these are added racist-sexist myths exploited for profit, from paranoid notions about Black sexuality to absurdities about Asian women as submissive receptacles.

A Major Debate

A major debate among feminists and civil libertarians has been how to chart an antiporn strategy without endangering freedom of expression. Some liberals—with the hearty support of the porn tycoons—maintain an absolutist position, insisting that any attack on pornography attacks the First Amendment.

It is true that antiporn legislation is a risky affair. Censorship laws have proven to come down hardest on progressive ideas, and can easily be used against the feminist movement itself

62

since right-wing ideologues, who control interpretation and enforcement of these laws, also consider homosexuality, birth control and non-marital sex "pornography." They can be depended upon to use antipornography laws against us.

Legislation, however, is not the only weapon. The Constitution, which guarantees free speech and provides protection from governmental interference, doesn't prohibit private actions and

WIDENING FRACTURES

protests. On the contrary, critics have a First Amendment right to organize against porn, just as we have a First Amendment right to organize against the Klan or Nazis and their chilling propaganda, although other liberals may label us uptight, moralistic prudes.

What's prudish about stopping depictions of sexual violence? And who's liberated by viewing a Native American woman bound and raped by a white man as shown in the video game "Custer's Revenge?"

Furthermore, this accusation blurs the distinction between pornography and erotica. Not all erotica is porn. And erotica itself—which many feminists see as important in sexual expression—must be limited to what is not brutish, exploitative and physically dangerous, regardless of sex or sexual preference.

Sex Discrimination Amendment

A controversial Minneapolis attempt to outlaw pornography has once again ignited the debate over legal restraints. Radical feminists author Andrea Dworkin and law professor Catherine MacKinnon proposed legislation to allow civil suits against pornography traffickers if complainants can show that porn led to a sexual attack. The ordinance, narrowly passed by the city council in December, was vetoed by the mayor in January.

The amendment defines pornography as the "sexually explicit subordination of women, graphically depicted, whether in pictures or in word." But "subordination" has a vast number of possible interpretations. Civil libertarians have a legitimate objection to this too-broad definition.

Another not-so-legitimate objection to the ordinance is the lack of positive proof establishing pornography as a cause of sexual violence. Women know there is an intrinsic relationship between pornography and sexual violence. (For instance, last

---

Porn Ordinance is Shaky Law

It isn't just women versus pornographers. If women win the right to sue publishers and producers, then so could Jews, blacks, a long list of people who may be able to prove they have been harmed by books, movies, speeches or even records.

Ellen Goodman, *The Boston Globe*, 1984.

year's rape of a woman on a New Bedford pool table was preceded by a Hustler magazine photo spread of a gang rape on a bar pool table.) Proving this in a court of law, however, is another thing.

The Minneapolis ordinance's civil rights approach to pornography, as distinguished from older obscenity and zoning laws, is a new one and may well have some legal potential. Everyone has a basic civil right not to be subjected to propaganda that advocates or legitimizes degradation, oppression and violence.

Fundamental Division

However, a primary shortcoming of the Minneapolis sex discrimination amendment is that it defines pornography as victimizing women exclusively, since the bill's underlying political ideology is that of radical feminism, which sees conflict between women and men as innate and male supremacy as the fundamental division in society.

Dworkin, a leading ideologue of radical feminism, has written: "Men love death. . . . In male culture, slow murder is the heart of eros." Dworkin's futilist ideology identifies the wrong enemy, degrades men, and scorns the broad-based support that the feminist movement has built. As one young man testifying at the Minneapolis hearings protested, "If women have a right not to be portrayed as whores by nature, then men have a right not to be portrayed as rapists by nature."

Porn involves not just sexism, but racism and heterosexism in a capitalist culture.

The fundamental division in society is not sexual, between men and women, but economic, between workers who produce everything, and capitalists who exploit both male and female labor. Porn reinforces the capitalist system. None of us will be fully free of pornography and everything it stands for until we replace capitalism with a socialist economy which does not depend on dominance and degradation.

This does not mean we must wait until after the revolution to take on the pornography terrorists. So far, no one has come up with legislation that has more advantages than perils. But organizing, educating, boycotting and building militant demonstrations have already proven their worth. The video rape game, "Custer's Revenge," for example, was withdrawn from the market under direct pressure from the feminist and Native American movements. Feminists now need to mount a similar campaign to get the murderous movie "Snuff" off every market.

PROHIBITING DISCRIMINATION
Andrea Dworkin and Catherine Mackinnon

Andrea Dworkin is an antipornography activist and feminist writer. Catherine Mackinnon is a feminist and law professor at the University of Minnesota. They wrote the controversial Minneapolis antipornography ordinance which defines pornography as a violation of women's civil rights.

Points To Consider

1. How is pornography defined?
2. In what ways does pornography hurt women?
3. What is the nature of the authors' antipornography ordinance?

Excerpted from a paper presented to the Minneapolis City Council, December 26, 1983.

*We learned that exposure to pornography
increases male aggression toward women
and leads men to see women as things, less
than human, and wanting and liking rape and
torture and humiliation.*

This ordinance defines pornography for what it is. Its central feature is that it subordinates women through sex . . .

The use of women in pornography and the impact of pornography on women's status and treatment is the primary focus of this ordinance. Pornography promotes environmental terrorism and private abuse of women and girls and, to a lesser extent, men and boys and transexuals. Society's efforts toward the civil and sexual equality of women and men are severely hampered—frankly, nearly destroyed—by the success of pornography. Most frequently, the pornography promotes rape, pain, humiliation and inferiority as experiences that are sexually pleasing to all women because we are women. The studies show that it is not atypical for men to believe and act on the pornography. Each time men are sexually aroused by pornography—the sexually explicit subordination of women—they learn to connect women's sexual pleasure to abuse and women's sexual nature to inferiority . . .

What We Have Learned

We learned that pornography is used in sexual assaults and to plan the sexual assaults. We learned that exposure to pornography increases male aggression toward women and leads men to see women as things, less than human, and wanting and liking rape and torture and humiliation. We also learned that pornography has been used to, and has the effect of, terrorizing women in their homes, in their neighborhoods, and in their places of work. We learned that pornography is used in relationships that range from the intimate to the anonymous in ways that give women no choice about seeing the pornography or doing the sex.

The purpose of the ordinance is to make available an effective remedy to those who choose to use it, so that women need no longer be paralyzed or passive or held back by the lack of a legitimate avenue for redress in the face of pornography—the systematic discrimination, the condoned brutality, and the glorified debasement that defines the condition of an entire group of people.

A Form of Discrimination

Pornography is a form of discrimination on the basis of sex. Pornography is the sexually explicit subordination of women, graphically depicted, whether in pictures or in words, that also includes one or more of the following:

(1) women are presented as sexual objects, things, or commodities; or

(2) women are presented as sexual objects who enjoy pain or humiliation; or

(3) women are presented as sexual objects who experience sexual pleasure in being raped; or

(4) women are presented as sexual objects tied up or cut up or mutilated or bruised or physically hurt; or

(5) women are presented in postures of sexual submission; or

(6) women's body parts—including but not limited to vaginas, breasts, and buttocks—are exhibited, such that women are reduced to those parts or such that the subordinate sexual status of women is reinforced; or

(7) women are presented as whores by nature; or

(8) women are presented being penetrated by objects or animals; or

(9) women are presented in scenarios of degradation, injury, abasement, torture, shown as filthy or inferior, bleeding, bruised, or hurt in a context that makes these conditions sexual.

Minneapolis City Ordinance, 1983.

How the Ordinance Would Work.

Like any other law that prohibits discrimination, this law would make available the administrative apparatus of the Human Rights Commission and the courts to adjudicate complaints. Once the law goes into effect, a person who has been coerced into a pornographic performance, had pornography forced on them, or has been assaulted or physically attacked or injured in a way directly caused by a specific piece of pornography could choose to complain to the Commission or go directly to court. Any woman can also complain against traffickers in pornography. Because the data from the hearings show that pornography increases male aggression against women, the public availability of the pornography, as defined in the ordinance, is in and of itself a violation of women's rights to equal personhood and citizenship. The systematic sexual subordination of the pornography **is** the injury under this section of the act.

The Commission or the court would then see if the pornography complained of meets the definition of pornography in the statute. The definition of pornography in the statute states exactly what pornography is and does. it describes exactly the trafficking in women engaged in by the pornographers, which ranges from dehumanizing women as sexual things and commodities to torturing and maiming women as sexual acts.

PROTECTING FREE SPEECH
Donald M. Fraser

Donald M. Fraser is the Mayor of Minneapolis and a former congressman from Minnesota. In the following statement, he explains why he vetoed the anti-pornography civil rights ordinance.

Points To Consider

1. Why would the enforcement of the antipornography ordinance be difficult?
2. Why does the ordinance violate the First Amendment?

Excerpted from Mayor Fraser's letter to the Minneapolis City Council, January 5, 1984.

The remedy sought through the ordinance as drafted is neither appropriate nor enforceable within our cherished tradition and constitutionally protected right of free speech.

During the last week, people all over America have heard the voices of women in Minneapolis who deplore the pervasive images of women in subordinate roles which continue to define women as second-class citizens. By authoring and supporting an amendment to our municipal law which would identify pornography as a violation of the civil rights of women, feminist leaders in Minneapolis have attacked one aspect of the American culture which appears to covertly sanction violence against women.

The thoughtful discussion this proposed ordinance has evoked has been healthy for our community. The proponents have contributed new concepts through their skillful analysis of an issue rarely discussed in the public policy arena. They have brought the issue of pornography and its effects on women to national, if not international, attention. I applaud their leadership for social change. As the Mayor of Minneapolis responsible for the governance of this community, however, I must veto the Civil rights ordinance which was passed by the City Council last Friday.

The remedy sought through the ordinance as drafted is neither appropriate nor enforceable within our cherished tradition and constitutionally protected right of free speech. The definition of pornography in the ordinance is so broad and so vague as to make it impossible for a bookseller, movie theater operator or museum director to adjust his or her conduct in order to keep from running afoul of its proscriptions. The ordinance needs more analysis and redrafting before a final judgement can be made as to whether or not it would then represent sound public policy and should be adopted.

1. Enforcement

Under the ordinance the enforcement of the "trafficking" provision appears to be as follows:

A person buys an item at a store which he or she believes is pornographic. The buyer takes the item to the Civil Rights Department and makes a complaint. An investigator is assigned to determine the facts. If the investigator confirms that the material

Right-wing book burners. Some feminists argue Minneapolis antipornography bill is different from censorship proposals of reactionary forces like those above. But end result is same: giving another weapon to employers and government to go after women's, Black, and labor movements.

is being sold at the store and believes that it is pornographic, a recommendation of probable cause is made to the Civil Rights Director after first being reviewed by the City Attorney. If the Director finds probable cause, the matter is placed for hearing before a panel of the Civil Rights Commission. This panel consists of one lawyer and two laypersons. They hold a hearing and are empowered to issue an injunction and award damages.

If the store appeals the decision, the power of the Court is limited to determining whether there was substantial evidence to support the decision of the hearing panel. The Court does not retry the case.

What this says is that an administrative panel would decide what can be sold, distributed or shown in the City of Minneapolis. When issues of free speech are raised, granting the decision-making power to an administrative panel is troubling to me. Some might call it a Board of Censors.

The procedures which were established to enforce civil rights laws emphasize negotiation and conciliation. They appear to have no place in the enforcement of anti-pornography laws.

2. Relationship to First Amendment

To the extent that this ordinance would bar obscene material it is redundant, because obscene material is now prohibited by law. The ordinance is broader, though. It seeks to ban material that is not obscene under existing law. The ban would apply to material that meets two requirements: it must be a) sexually explicit and b) degrading to women. But sexually explicit material that is not obscene is protected by the First Amendment. Also protected is the expression of abhorrent or detestable ideas such as the claim that women are mere sex objects or otherwise to be thought of in degrading terms.

If sexually explicit material that is not obscene also degrades women, then does the protection of the First Amendment disappear? The answer is not free of doubt. A credible argument has been made that the effect of such material is to impair the full enjoyment by women of other rights. But more research and analysis is needed on this constitutional question.

As drafted, the ordinance is too broad and vague to give notice as to what non-obscene material would be prohibited. This is particularly important because the ordinance expressly precludes any defense that the defendant did not know or intend the material to be pornographic or discriminatory against women. The chilling effect of an overly broad ordinance is well known.

EXAMINING
COUNTERPOINTS

This activity may be used as an individualized study guide for students in libraries and resource centers or as a discussion catalyst in small group and classroom discussions.

The Point

Pornography has nothing to do with free speech, and first amendment rights should not be extended to pornographic publications.

The Counterpoint

Pornographic publications should not be censored in any democratic society.

Guidelines

Social issues are usually complex, but often problems become oversimplified in political debates and discussion. Usually a polarized version of social conflict does not adequately represent the diversity of views that surround social conflicts.

1. Examine the counterpoints above. Then write down other possible interpretations of this issue than the two arguments stated in the counterpoints above.

2. Do you agree more with the point or the counterpoint? Why?

3. Which opinion in this chapter best illustrates the point?

4. Which opinion best illustrates the counterpoint?

5. Do any cartoons in this chapter illustrate the meaning of the point or counterpoint arguments? Which ones and why?

CHAPTER 4

CHILD PORNOGRAPHY IN AMERICA
Debating the Issue

13

CHILD SEXUAL EXPLOITATION
Defining the Problem
Howard A. Davidson

Children are being sexually exploited throughout the country in a variety of ways. Most commonly, they are used as prostitutes or models for the production of pornographic photographs and films. This is distinguishable from another serious and related problem—sexual abuse of children by parents and guardians. Sexual **exploitation** usually involves a commercial element: children selling themselves or being sold as prostitutes or models. Sexual **abuse**, on the other hand, is generally perpetrated by an adult the child knows, most often by a parent, guardian or a person with authority over the child, and generally has no commercial element. While the two problems are interrelated (i.e., parents who sexually abuse their children may also exploit them commercially), this monograph will be concerned only with sexual exploitation.

Child pornography, also known as "kiddie porn," is generally defined as films, photographs, magazines, books and motion pictures which depict children in sexually explicit acts, both heterosexual and homosexual. Production, distribution and sale of child pornography is a secretive business, making a determination of its full extent extremely difficult. Estimates of the number of children involved range from the thousands to the hundreds

Excerpted from testimony before the U.S. Senate Subcommittee on Juvenile Justice, November 5, 1981. Howard A. Davidson was the Director of Child Advocacy and Protection for the American Bar Association when he made this testimony.

of thousands. The statistics cannot be accurately verified and the facts and figures vary, but one thing is clear: a significant number of children are being sexually exploited throughout the country.

The availability of child pornography is a good indicator of its nature and scope. A relatively obscure and unusual product as late as the 1960's, child pornography has become increasingly popular. In 1977, there were at least 260 different monthly magazines published in the United States with such names as "Torrid Tots," "Night Boys," "Lolita," "Boys Who Love Boys," and "Children Love."

Congress has concluded that child pornography and child prostitution have become highly organized industries that operate on a nationwide scale. It has been estimated that these enterprises may gross a half-billion to a billion dollars a year. To date, police have uncovered production centers in Los Angeles, New York, Chicago and several other large cities. But production is by no means limited to these areas. Police have also discovered child pornography and prostitution operations in suburban and rural communities. Moreover, since such photographs or films can be taken in private homes, discovery of their production is very difficult.

Child pornography is a lucrative business; the costs of sexually exploiting children are minimal and the profits enormous. A magazine that retails for $7.50 to $12.50 per copy can be produced for as little as 35 to 50 cents. Similarly, a cheap home movie camera can be used to produce films that sell thousands of copies for $75 to $200 each. These prices are considerably higher than for similar materials featuring adult pornography.

Child Pornography and Child Prostitution

Several authorities have found a close relationship between child pornography and child prostitution. Frequently, a person hiring a child prostitute will also film their activities. These films are then reproduced and sold to distributors.

There have also been cases where child pornography and prostitution operations have been organized into "sex rings." For example, a Tennessee minister who operated a home for wayward boys encouraged the boys to engage in orgies. He then filmed them with hidden cameras and sold the films. Also, he arranged for "sponsors" to come to the home and have sex with the boys.

However, child pornography is generally a "cottage industry," with production occurring surreptitiously in private homes and motel rooms. Consequently, combatting the problem and protecting the children can be very difficult.

Profile of People Who Sexually Exploit Children

The rapid growth of child pornography reveals a demand for the material by people who are stimulated by sexual activity with children. They are known as "pedophiles"—people who are predisposed to sexually use children or who turn to them as a result of conflicts or problems in their adult relationships. Some have organized and become vocal about what they believe is their right to sexual fulfillment . . .

The pedophile's sexual access to children is gained by either pressuring the child into sexual activity through enticement, encouragement, or instruction, or by forcing such activity through threat, intimidation, or physical duress. However, pedophiles usually seek to control children rather than injure them . . .

Profile of the Exploited Child

Child pornographers have little difficulty recruiting youngsters. Typically, the victims are runaways who come to the city with little or no money. A recent U.S. Senate Committee report estimates that between 700,000 to one million children run away from home each year. Adult exploiters pick them up at bus stations, hamburger stands and street corners and offer them money, gifts or drugs for sexual favors.

However, not all exploited children are runaways. Many seem to live normal lives with their families. Frequently, they are children who have been abused at home or come from broken homes or live with parents who simply don't care about their activities. The Senate Committee Report suggested the following characteristics as typical of a sexually exploited boy:
—Between the ages of 8 and 17
—An under achiever in school or at home
—Usually without previous homosexual experience
—Came from a home where the parents were absent either physically or psychologically
—Had no strong moral or religious obligations
—Usually had no record of previous delinquency
—Suffered from poor sociological development
Often the parents are unaware of what their children are doing, but there have been cases where parents have sold their own children for sexual purposes.

The effects of sexual exploitation on children are devastating. Many children suffer physical harm as a result of the premature and inappropriate sexual demands placed on them. Perhaps more serious is the disruption of emotional development. Although the psychological problems experienced by children who are sexually exploited have not been extensively studied, there is ample evidence that such involvement is harmful. One recent study suggests that children who are used to produce pornography suffer harmful effects similar to those experienced by incest victims. Such effects may include depression, guilt and psychologically induced somatic disorders. Often, these children grow up to lead a life of drugs and prostitution. More tragically, children who are sexually abused are more likely to abuse their own children.

(Editor's Note: The following readings debate the constitutional merits of laws that attempt to regulate the distribution of child pornography.)

A PLAN TO ELIMINATE CHILD PORNOGRAPHY
Phyllis Schlafly

Phyllis Schlafly is the author and publisher of the Eagle Forum *newsletter and the* Phyllis Schlafly Report. *She has been a national conservative leader in opposing the equal rights amendment and supporting other conservative causes.*

Points To Consider

1. Why have laws against child pornography been ineffective?
2. What was the meaning of **New York V. Ferber**?
3. What plan is advocated to eliminate child pornography?
4. Do you agree with this plan? Why or why not?

Phyllis Schlafly, "New Weapons in the Battle Against Pornography," **The Phyllis Schlafly Report**, June, 1984.

The so-called intellectual self-proclaimed "civil libertarians" thus rushed to the rescue of those dregs of humanity who deliberately lead children into lives of sin and depravity.

President Ronald Reagan signed the Child Protection Act into law on May 21, 1984—a new Federal law designed to wipe out the evil of child pornography. This was a great day for all those who believe in fundamental decency, and a rewarding day for Eagle Forum which has been working for the passage of this law since the opportunity was opened up by the Supreme Court decision in *New York v. Ferber* on July 2, 1982.

As the President said that day in the Rose Garden, "There is no one lower or more vicious than a person who would profit from the abuse of children, whether by using them in pornographic material or by encouraging their sexual abuse by distributing this material." The 1982 *Ferber* decision combined with the 1984 statute constitute a stunning affirmation by our society that there is NO First Amendment right to take pictures of children in pornographic poses.

Child pornography is the use of children under age 18 in pictures, books or films to perform sex acts, or to pose in lewd positions or circumstances. The new Federal statute increases penalties on offenders tenfold, and gives prosecutors additional law enforcement powers such as the power to get wiretaps and to seize the profits, pictures and equipment of the pornographers.

The New Bill

Far more important than the raising of the penalties, however, is the way the new bill eliminates the reason why, for the last 15 years, police have seldom bothered to arrest porn-peddlers, and prosecuting attorneys have seldom bothered to prosecute. That reason has been their belief that their work will be for naught because the courts will reverse all convictions after the porn lawyers wrap the smut-peddlers in the First Amendment.

Beginning in the mid-1960s, the Supreme Court tied the hands of the police and the prosecutors by requiring any conviction to meet a highly-contrived and almost impossible definition of obscenity. Under the Supreme Court rulings, nothing could be judged "obscene" unless it was "utterly without redeeming social value."

So, the high-priced porn lawyers outdid themselves in arguing that a shred of "social value" on a half-page of a book, or in fleeting episodes in a movie, should justify a full-length book or movie of shocking depravity. If the porn lawyers could argue that the material had one iota of "serious" literary, artistic or political content, then the pornography and its peddlers would be protected by the First Amendment.

The Supreme Court opened up a real opportunity for effective prosecution and conviction in *New York v. Ferber.* The Court unanimously held that "the prevention of the sexual exploitation and abuse of children constitutes a governmental objective of surpassing importance" and that child pornography is **not** protected by the First Amendment.

The New York law upheld in the *Ferber* decision prohibits **any** pictures of children in sexual conduct or in lewd positions or circumstances. To obtain a conviction, prosecuting attorneys now need show only that the materials portray under-age children in sexual poses.

At the time of the decision, only 20 states had the strong New York-type law upheld in the *Ferber* case. The remaining 30 states and the Federal Government had weaker laws that were virtually unenforceable because the child pornography convictions were forced to meet the difficult legal definition of "obscenity."

Once the Supreme Court gave the green light, Eagle Forum lobbied strong child porn bills through many state legislatures and city councils. The public demand became overwhelming; the Child Protection Act passed the U.S. House by 400 to 1.

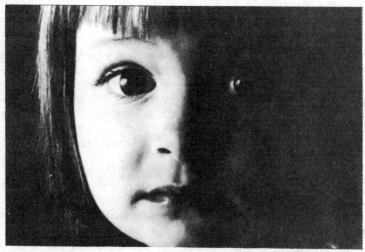

National Committee To Prevent Child Abuse

Child Porn Ring In California

A computerized, international child pornography ring involving girls who were seduced with promises of household jobs has been uncovered after operating for about 10 years, police said Friday . . .

"We have mailing lists, customer lists from all over the country. Whatever your delight would be, you could write in and say, 'I would like these kinds of pictures' and they would fill the bill."

He said the operation was so big that two home computers were used to keep customer records.

Associated Press, April 7, 1984.

The National Debate

One of the most interesting features of this national debate over the last years is the line-up of players in the legislative battles to pass stronger laws. Contrary to what one might expect, the chief witnesses against the child pornography bill were not the pornographers (who were hiding somewhere under a rock), but the American Civil Liberties Union (which always litigates in behalf of a radical interpretation of the First Amendment) and the librarians (who asked for a privileged exemption from laws against child pornography).

The so-called intellectual self-proclaimed "civil libertarians" thus rushed to the rescue of those dregs of humanity who deliberately lead children into lives of sin and depravity. The intellectuals minimized and trivialized the horror of the crime by labeling it merely "kiddie porn." The liberal lawyers wove a web of "freedom of press" and "civil liberties" slogans under which the children were exposed naked to the commercial cameras filming their private little parts and unnatural acts, while their exploiters were clothed in the sacred mantle of the First Amendment.

The sexploitation of children is such a hideous variety of child abuse that the strongest laws against child pornography should be written and enforced against everyone, including bookstores, theaters, schools, and libraries. The selling or displaying of children in sexual acts or lewd positions cannot be tolerated by a civilized society. Prosecutions should be vigorously pushed by all the U.S. District Attorneys under the new statute.

EDUCATE ABOUT HUMAN SEXUALITY
Larry Flynt

Larry Flynt is the publisher of Hustler *magazine. The author makes his living by selling pornography and presented the following statements before a congressional committee.*

Points To Consider

1. How does Larry Flynt describe child pornography?
2. What does he say about the First Amendment?
3. When will we begin to better understand human sexuality?

Excerpted from testimony by Larry Flynt before the House Subcommittee on Crime, September 20, 1977.

It just horrifies me at the thought of the first amendment getting dragged into another murky situation. I feel that somehow we must deal with child abuse and sexual exploitation of children through child abuse laws and not involve the first amendment.

First of all, I would like to state at the outset that I am opposed to child abuse or the exploitation of children in any manner.

But I am here today because I am not only concerned about it, I am concerned about the first amendment implications as well.

This morning I picked up a copy of the New York magazine and on the cover of that magazine they have a woman and her daughter, and it says "Meet Terry and Brooke Shields. Brooke is 12, she poses nude; Terry is her mother, she thinks it is swell." New York is a very respected magazine. This is about a movie that this 12-year-old girl appears in.

I am not going to elaborate on if the movie meets the criteria of the Federal obscenity statute. But I do feel New York magazine is constitutionally protected, has a constitutional right to publish this article. And this is what I am concerned about, with the legislation being considered as it is. It just horrifies me at the thought of the first amendment getting dragged into another murky situation. And I see this happening. I feel that somehow we must deal with child abuse and sexual exploitation of children through child abuse laws and not involve the first amendment.

I don't know if this is possible, but rather than legislation, I think there is a need for better understanding of human sexuality. I don't feel that legislation is going to be the answer. There is probably not anyone in the world that is more familiar with pornography than I am.

Pornography Is My Business

From a professional point of view, pornography is my business. And I have over 10 million readers of my magazine, it is a combined readership, over 50 million. The majority of the letters that come into my magazine are from people that would like to see photographs of shaved genitalia. What they are really asking for is photographs of children, but they can't come out and say it.

There are millions of these dirty little old men out there, and legislation is not going to help it, it is going to make it worse.

85

I think we must direct our energies to a better understanding of why these problems happen in society.

At the turn of the century we had 50 million people in this country; we have 250 million people now. Our cultural evolution has forced changes, but we must be receptive to them. The Judeo-Christian ethnic, as it exists today, has created more neurotics in society than any other single factor. I do not say this as an atheist, but as a man who believes in God, but a just God, and I think that an individual has to find Him within himself. I think after all of the rhetoric and all that is said in the Scripture, the only thing He ever really intended was for us to live fairly with one another. If we don't get the church out of the business of drafting legislation, we are not going to have a world to live in.

Many of the people who are going to be affected by the laws, and I am talking about people who would be prosecuted, they really need medical help more than imprisonment.

You know, we spend millions and millions of dollars to try to get a better understanding of the diseases like cancer, heart disease, the common killers, so we can know something about them and do something about them. When it comes to human sexuality, nobody seems to want to spend any money or to find anything out. Most people know more about changing a flat tire than they do about human sexuality.

It is absolutely essential. We use it to communicate with more than any other medium today, yet is is the only medium of communication not protected by the first amendment. Marijuana seems to be tolerated to a certain degree in society today. The statistics indicate that over 18 million people use it, many States are passing legislation to decriminalize it. I see this happening probably because everybody was doing it, so as a society we are going to condone it.

Are we going to condone child abuse, sexual exploitation of children, because everybody is doing it?

Gentlemen, in all due respect, I submit that there are millions, not a handful, millions of people out there that are turned on by children and want to see them exploited sexually. It is sad, but it exists.

It exists because of the paradoxical society we live in, and all of the years of hypocrisy and inconsistency. The biggest reason for this, and this is medically, but I would hope the committee would look into it, is that the men appear to be more fascinated with genitalia and nudism than women. Playgirl magazine hasn't had any success. The reason for this is because the genital area is the most tabooed part of the female body; it is what the ankle was 30 years ago. And when it is on a child or an adolescent, it is even more fascinating.

Women grow up with children, most often women are helping raise little brother or little sister, helping raise their own children, and they have a lot of contact with them, a lot of exposure to nudity. You find the female doesn't have these hang-ups and these difficulties that the males do.

Repressive Laws

So when you pass laws that make it even more repressive, you are really perpetuating a problem rather than doing anything about it.

I am not saying we don't need this legislation. I think we have to be very careful about it. It is a question of people having an awfully lot of preconceived ideas.

We just simply can not, can not approach this problem out of emotion. We must do it out of knowledge. Many people could say I am here because I make a lot of money on pornography. I tried to give some of that money to our President to establish a Commission for this purpose. He would not accept it. I can understand probably the reasons why he couldn't. I am prepared today to turn all of my profits and future profits of Hustler magazine over to this committee or a new Commission that would be set up to study child abuse and the prevention of it, because it is more important to me than the money involved, because if my theories, and the theories of Dr. Prescott are correct, that means we are right, and everybody else is wrong, and society is 180 degrees out.

IMPLEMENT CHILD
PROTECTION LAWS
William J. Hughes

William J. Hughes is a Democratic congressman from New Jersey. He is currently Chairman of the House Subcommittee on Crime of the Committee on the Judiciary.

Points To Consider:

1. What is the nature of child sexual exploitation?
2. What is the 1977 law and how effective has it been?
3. How can laws protecting children from sexual exploitation be improved?

Excerpted from a statement by William J. Hughes before the House Subcommittee on Crime, June 16, 1983.

Once I even heard child pornography referred to as a 'victimless' crime. That's nonsense. There are, by one account, over a half a million children in this country used in sex-for-sale activities.

This is a hearing I'd much prefer not to be holding. Crime is never a pretty subject, but we encounter few crimes as ugly as that which we are looking at today—sexual abuse of children.

Sexual Exploitation of Children

Six years ago, Congress enacted legislation to combat one particular form of sexual child abuse. This was the disgusting—and increasing—practice of sexual exploitation of children by inducing them to engage in sex acts, frequently with adults, in order to photograph and film them and to distribute these pornographic products to persons interested in viewing these perversities. Testimony before the subcommittee on crime at that time indicated that thousands of children are being abused in this fashion. We learned that these child abusers produce their own magazines and newsletters devoted to these practices. They exchange photos, films, publications, and sometimes, the children themselves. They develop their own trade lingo under which young boys are known as "chickens", and depraved men who prey upon them are "chicken hawks". We even heard from individual groups who claimed that explicit sex by children, including very young children, is healthy if not essential to their development. One offered as the letterhead of its stationery, apparently in complete seriousness, a depiction of a child undressing with the slogan "sex before eight (meaning years old) or it's too late" (meaning for proper development). This argument, like the photographic materials which are the product of the inducement of children to engage in explicit sex acts, is rubbish. I agree with the observation of news commentator Bill Moyers, who stated in a recent editorial:

"Once I even heard child pornography referred to as a 'victimless' crime. That's nonsense. There are, by one account, over a half a million children in this country used in sex-for-sale activities. Some films have been made with children under four. No victims?"

Our Purpose

The purpose of our hearing today will be to get a progress report on the effectiveness of the 1977 law in facilitating prosecution of these child abusers and in drying up the supply of the child pornography materials they produce. We will also be taking testimony aimed at identifying the nature of the child pornography "industry" and developing a profile of the typical child at risk of such exploitation.

Improving The Law

Finally, and most important, we will be looking at proposals to strengthen the law already on the books. It is encouraging to learn that there have been several dozen successful prosecutions

By David Seavey, USA TODAY

FBI Uncovers Child-Stealing Sex Ring

The FBI has uncovered a nationwide kidnapping ring that specializes in abducting children—primarily young boys—and selling them here and abroad for the purposes of sex and pornography.

Evidence developed by a special task force has revealed that the ring accepts orders from customers based on height, weight and hair color, and then steals children as young as 3 years old who fit the descriptions.

St. Paul Pioneer Press, December 22, 1983.

under this law for distribution of child pornography materials. At the same time, I was very disappointed to learn that there has not been a single conviction under the principal provision of the 1977 law, which is aimed at the persons directly abusing children by posing them for such films and photographs. We want to learn why we have been unable to reach these principal perpetrators of sexual child abuse, and we want to look at other ways to make the federal law more effective in stopping sexual child abuse and the proliferation of materials depicting that abuse. The United States Supreme Court last year cleared the way for broader and more effective use of laws of this nature when it held that child pornography materials are entitled to no constitutional protection under the first amendment. As a result of that decision, one of the changes in the law we'll be looking at would permit the prosecution of persons distributing such materials without proving that the materials are legally obscene.

DON'T TRAMPLE THE FIRST AMENDMENT
Heather Florence

While testifying before a congressional committee, the author described herself as follows: "I am an attorney in private practice in New York as a member of the law firm of Lankenau Kovner & Bickford. I sit as a member of the ACLU's Communications Media Committee, which studies current issues with impact on First Amendment rights."

Points To Consider

1. How should child pornography be dealt with?
2. What kind of laws should be avoided?
3. Why does the author oppose laws prohibiting the dissemination of child pornography?

Excerpted from testimony by Heather Florence before the House Subcommittee on Crime, June 10, 1977.

However unlawful the sexual exploitation of children for commercial purposes may be, the Constitution requires that any legislation designed to cure these evils not trample on First Amendment rights in the process.

I do want to clarify at the outset that to the extent there is a problem, such as you have heard testified about today, the American Civil Liberties Union certainly believes that the existing laws to prevent the abuse of children should be effectively enforced, and would hope that the States and this Congress, if appropriate, can enact further legislation to protect children from abuse, whether it be sexual abuse for commercial purposes or not . . .

The Problem

The problem of "child pornography" or "kiddie porn", as it has been dubbed by the press, has recently come to the attention of the ACLU which, after much consideration, has developed views on the issue which I shall be articulating here today. In discussing the issue, generally, I shy away from the phrase "child porn" as that confuses two distinct issues—child abuse which is unlawful activity and the dissemination of printed or visual materials which is constitutionally protected.

The problem we are discussing today is a difficult one, not only for society and for this Congress, but also for the ACLU. For, unlike many issues on which the ACLU speaks out, it fully supports the purpose of the proposed legislation. The ACLU wholeheartedly joins with the many legislators, private individuals and community groups in condemning the sexual exploitation of children for any purpose, including commercial purposes. The actions of those responsible for these abuses are reprehensible. The ACLU believes, and strongly urges, that criminal laws prohibiting child abuse and contributing to the delinquency of a minor should be vigorously enforced, and if appropriate and useful, enhanced in order to eliminate this repugnant activity. So long as the imposition of criminal penalties upon those responsible for the sexual exploitation of children is done with the constitutionally-required due process, it raises no civil liberties problems and will be fully supported by the ACLU.

Yet, however unlawful the sexual exploitation of children for commercial purposes may be, and however repugnant the resulting materials may be, the Constitution requires that any legislation designed to cure these evils not trample on First Amendment rights in the process.

The ACLU's basic position is that while it is perfectly proper to prosecute those who engage in illegal action, constitutionally protected speech cannot be the vehicle. Accordingly, the ACLU submits that those who directly cause and induce a minor to engage in a sexual act, or engage in it with a minor, are those who violate the laws; those who recruit and offer children for sexual acts clearly should be prosecuted. Indeed, the ACLU believes that even the activities of one who records the event of the sexual behavior, such as the photographer at the scene, can be found within the group of persons who have caused the act to occur. In contrast, those who have not participated in causing or engaging in the sexual activity but who may profit as a result of it, such as a publisher, editor, distributor or retailer, are not violating the law. While we may vigorously dislike and reject what they do, their activities in publishing and disseminating printed or visual materials are wholly protected by the First Amendment . . .

One of the things we hope we can be helpful with is obviously if you end up passing an unconstitutional bill because it does violate first amendment rights, in addition to the Civil Liberties Union and other people getting exercised about that, you are going to find yourself without an effective law to do what should be done . . .

We do that not just because we don't want you to step on first amendment rights, but because we think it is important that legislation passed in the area be effective, and that when the first, second or third person is arrested under it and prosecution begins, you don't find the whole thing thrown out and dismissed on the basis of an unconstitutional statute . . .

I am sure it would strike you as an inept analogy, but I do think it's useful to think of the Pentagon papers case.

Granted that material is very different from what we are talking about today, there was an instance where the Supreme Court acknowledged in the opinion that there might have been criminal activity involved in obtaining these documents.

There was, you know, just theft, larceny problems, perhaps under the Espionage Act, but the material itself could not be restrained and its publication should not be punished.

So, we feel that the fact there was illegal activity, does not provide a basis for punishing those who simply disseminated the material.

Second, to the extent material portrays child abuse or engaging in sexual acts with children as attractive or desirable activity, as offensive as we find that, again, we feel that the law is quite clear, that you cannot prohibit the mailing of the material or the obtaining of the material for those reasons . . .

My Own Feeling

I guess my own feeling on the pornography issue overall, and I believe to a certain extent this does reflect the views of the ACLU, and, indeed, as was stated by Mr. Leonard of the District Attorneys Association earlier today, we believe little purpose is served by the obscenity laws as they currently exist, and that people are going to want this material and they are going to manage to get it and to the extent there has been substantial infiltration by organized crime, as has been testified to here today, that infiltration probably is going to be the result of the fact that it is considered contraband, and that there are risks attendent to it.

Whether this particular legislation or some version of it would have an effect on the industry itself, my hunch would be the largest effect it would have, at least in the first instance, until enforcement is fully under swing, is to increase the involvement of organized crime.

Because it becomes much more difficult to get, the people don't want to take the risk, so instead of having legitimate businessmen engaged in it, it's even more likely to go underground more than it is. Now, that is presupposing a law on the books and questionable enforcement.

We have always tried to think of other things this committee might consider to get at the heart of the problem, and the heart of the problem is, of course, the abuse of the children themselves.

A thought we have come up with, would be some kind of amendment to the Child Abuse Prevention and Treatment Act, that sets up a center to study child abuse treatment.

I would be very happy to answer any questions that my comments have raised. I do want to emphasize that the American Civil Liberties Union in general, and I, of course, personally, would welcome the opportunity to continue to work with the committee and to give you the benefit of our thoughts in the area.

RECOGNIZING AUTHOR'S POINT OF VIEW

This activity may be used as an individualized study guide for students in libraries and resource centers or as a discussion catalyst in small group and classroom discussions.

The capacity to recognize an author's point of view is an essential reading skill. Many readers do not make clear distinctions between descriptive articles that relate factual information and articles that express a point of view. Think about the readings in chapter four. Are these readings essentially descriptive articles that relate factual information or articles that attempt to persuade through editorial commentary and analysis?

Guidelines

1. Read through the following source descriptions. Choose one of the source descriptions that best describes each reading in chapter four.

   Source Descriptions
   a. **Essentially an article that relates factual information**
   b. **Essentially an article that expresses editorial points of view**
   c. **Both of the above**
   d. **None of the above**

2. After careful consideration, pick out one source that you agree with the most. Be prepared to explain the reasons for your choice in a general class discussion.

3. Choose one of the source descriptions above that best describes the other readings in this book.

CHAPTER 5

PORNOGRAPHY IN FOREIGN NATIONS
Global Perspectives

PORNOGRAPHY IN FOREIGN NATIONS:
Global Perspectives

Chapter Overview

This chapter allows readers to look at pornography in selected foreign countries. It also permits an interesting comparison of pornography in Western and democratic nations with the Soviet Union and socialist countries. Very little information is presented by American and Western social scientists about the nature and treatment of pornography in socialist economic systems.

The selections by Berl Kutchinsky and Judith Bat-Ada provide another comparison with their conflicting views on the relationship of pornography and sexual violence. Kutchinsky believes no strong evidence exists to link pornography to the increase of sexual crimes and violence. He points out that rape, for example, has declined in West Germany and cites data showing that repeal of censorship laws in Denmark may have led to a decrease of some sexual crimes. In her article on Israel, however, Judith Bat-Ada is representative of some leading feminist writers who claim that a direct link exists between pornography and sexual violence against women.

TRADITIONAL AND MODERN PORNOGRAPHY IN EUROPE
Berl Kutchinsky

Berl Kutchinsky is a social scientist and researcher associated with the Institute of Criminal Science at the University of Copenhagen. The following statement is excerpted from his controversial study explaining the decrease in registered sex crimes in Copenhagen. The author says that research still supports the findings of the 1970 Commission on Pornography and Obscenity that pornography is basically harmless and can have positive benefits.

Points To Consider

1. What was traditional European pornography like?
2. How does modern pornography differ from traditional?
3. What is the relationship between pornography and rape?
4. Does pornography have a role in crime control?

"Obscenity and Pornography: Behavioral Aspects" by Berl Kutchinsky. Excerpted with permission of the publisher from the ENCYCLOPEDIA OF CRIME AND JUSTICE, Sanford H. Kadish, Editor in Chief. Volume 3, pages 1078–1085. Copyright © 1983 by The Free Press, a Division of Macmillan, Inc.

Besides being basically harmless, pornography may indeed have positive benefits as an instrument of crime control.

Traditional European Pornography

Although erotic art seems to be as universal as sex and art, the kind of commercialized hard-core pornography familiar in the late twentieth century appeared relatively recently in the history of the Western world. The beginnings of the prelegalization period of pornography can be traced rather precisely to the decade of the 1650s, when three pornographic classics were published: *La puttana errante, L'Ecole des filles,* and *Satyra sotadica* (Foxon). These books were soon translated into all the major languages and became the models of all later pornographic books (and, indeed, of twentieth-century pornographic photographs and films). One finds in them lesbianism, sodomy, seduction, multiple copulation, flagellation, and sadism—as well as total amorality, a disregard for artistic merit, an absence of affection or other emotions, flimsy plots, stereotyped characterizations, monotonous repetitiousness, and a constant exaggeration of sexual interest, energy, and potency.

Before 1960, pornographic books were published mainly in Paris, Brussels, Rome, Leipzig, and (since 1846) New York. Pornographic films, introduced in the early twentieth century, were produced in Japan, Cuba, and South America.

The Modern Pornography Wave

Since about 1960, pornography has become much more visible. Whereas the early pornography consisted mostly of printed texts, with occasional pictures, it increasingly became chiefly pictorial. In addition, its quantity increased, it became cheaper, it was widely advertised and publicized (in part because of obscenity trials and antismut campaigns), and it became more and more acceptable to the dominant classes and professions, as well as to the authorities. As a consequence, for the first time in history pornography became accessible to the common man.

One important factor facilitating this wave of pornography has been the development of new technologies for the mass production of color magazines of high technical quality at very low cost. No doubt the most important element, however, has been the emergence of a liberalized view of sexual behavior. This so-called sexual revolution—with an unmistakable Western capitalist slant of passive, somewhat alienated consumerism—has been influential in several ways. It has awakened and strengthened a latent need for erotic stimulants among many people, has made possible the economic exploitation of this new attitude, and has paved the way for more lenient law enforcement (and often the eventual abolition of bans) with respect to sexual behavior. The mass media played an indispensable role in this particular area of the sexual revolution, serving as intermediary between producers, consumers, and the authorities. Secularization—the declining influence of the churches and of religion in social and political life—was also significant.

The first countries to experience the early stages of the modern pornography wave were Denmark and Sweden. They were the first in 1969 and 1970, to repeal all restrictions on the sale of pornography to consenting adults. Denmark and Sweden accordingly became the main international suppliers of hard-core pornographic magazines and, to a lesser extent, of 8-mm films. After 1970 the wave climaxed and receded in these two countries, but it rolled on to engulf others. By 1980, hardly a country in the Western world had not experienced at least the early stages of a pornography wave.

Soft-Core Wave

A highly complex social phenomenon, a pornography wave within a single country can be divided into distinct stages. The first stage is usually marked by the abolition of all restrictions against nonpictorial pornography. Almost simultaneously, the traditional "girlie" magazines become more risqué: pubic hair and, later, genitals are shown, and eventually, photographs of two women or a woman and a man engaging in simulated foreplay. Soft-core magazines specializing in sadomasochistic or "bondage" themes appear. Many magazines carry "contact advertisements" (often simply prostitutes' offers of their services), as well as advertisements for the mail-order sale of contraceptives and pornographic products. The soft-core magazines produced during this stage of the pornography wave are often rather primitive despite their efforts to imitate such sophisticated competitors as *Playboy* and *Penthouse*, which are published in several languages.

The Transition

The transition from the soft-core to the hard-core stage of a pornography wave may be quite gradual. Nevertheless, by standards widely accepted in the trade, the hard-core stage is reached when explicit photographs of active sexual organs are shown. In Denmark and Sweden this stage was reached in 1967,

101

two years before pictorial pornography was actually legalized. Initially publishing black-and-white photographs of couples engaged in coitus, these magazines began to feature high-quality color photographs and group-sex scenes in 1968 and 1969— while prosecutions ground to a halt and sales figures soared.

The stage of nondeviant hard-core pornography was reached in the other Scandinavian countries and the Central European countries in the early 1970s, although only West Germany actually legalized such material. This stage was reached in most Southern European countries in the late 1970s. In Great Britain and Ireland, however, hard-core pornography remained essentially an expensive imported commodity, sold at some risk under the counter, well into the 1980s. The availability of such material varied considerably from one part of Australia, New Zealand, and Canada to another . . .

Aggressive Pornography and Rape

One looks in vain even for documentation that growth in exposure to aggressive pornography was indeed accompanied or followed by an equal growth in the incidence of forcible-rape— although even to establish such a temporal link would not prove causality . . .

Between 1960 and 1969 the number of forcible rapes in the United States increased from 9.4 per 100,000 to 18.1 per 100,000—a total change of 93 percent, with an annual average of 10.3 percent. Although this was a sizable increase, it was actually lower than the rate of growth for four of the six serious crimes on the Federal Bureau of Investigation's Crime Index. During these years much soft-core and some hard-core pornography was available, but very little of the aggressive variety. The Obscenity Commission correctly concluded that the rising incidence of rape was part of a general pattern of increasing crime in the United States and as such represented no evidence of the influence of pornography. . . .

Rape statistics in other countries where pornography—especially aggressive pornography—is easily obtainable produce results even more devastating to claimed links between pornography and rape. In West Germany the rape rates remained remarkably steady, in fact with a slight decrease, amounting to 6 percent, between 1972 and 1979—and in 1973 most forms of pornography were legalized, with aggressive pornography (still illegal) being easily accessible.

In sum, it is quite difficult to justify the extensive laboratory research on aggressive pornography and its possible links to rape . . . It can, of course, be claimed that the adverse effects of pornography are cumulative and will manifest themselves in the
102

future. Although this possibility cannot be totally excluded, it is not plausible. It would seem as if a great many researchers have been attempting to discover complicated psychological explanations of causal relations that do not exist.

Pornography and Crime Control

Besides being basically harmless, pornography may indeed have positive benefits as an instrument of crime control. Unfortunately, the lack of academic respectability attached to the subject has tended to block empirical investigation of this possibility—the fifth of the possible relationships between crime and pornography . . .

Many psychiatrists and clinical psychologists believe that potential sex offenders use pornography in order to obtain a noncriminal sexual outlet—that is, fantasy and masturbation (Kronhausen and Kronhausen; Committee on Obscenity and Film Censorship). It is therefore hypothesized that the greater the opportunity potential offenders have to obtain pornography, the more they will be diverted away from committing sexual offenses.

This hypothesis does not extend to forcible rape: there is no evidence that rape can be prevented by making pornography available to the would-be-rapist as a surrogate. However, studies in Denmark show that the actual incidence of voyeurism and "physical indecency toward girls" (that is, child molesting) declined sharply between 1967 and 1973—precisely the years in which all forms of pornography became readily available. Complex and detailed analysis of the evidence seems to indicate that pornography may be useful in treating the psychological and sexual dysfunctions of child molesters, individuals who turn to children because they are unable to establish normal sexual relations with mature girls and women.

The question of whether uncontrolled exposure to pornography may reduce the incidence of child molesting and possibly of such other offenses as voyeurism requires further research in other countries.

19

GLOBAL PERSPECTIVES

PORN IN THE PROMISED LAND
Judith Bat-Ada

*Dr. Judith Bat-Ada is director of the Institute for the Study
of Media and the Family, an educative and investigative
organization concerned with the effect of anti-female
image/information upon the life and liberty of women and
children in Israel.*

Points To Consider

1. What does pornography mean?
2. How does pornography relate to violence?
3. What does the author say about the "Denmark data" on pornography?
4. What is the major difference between Israeli and American pornography?

Judith Bat-Ada, "Porn in the Promised Land," **Lilith,** Fall/Winter, 1983,
pp. 9–14. Reprinted with permission of the author.

'The point about the relationship between pornography and rape is this: pornography, even at its most banal, objectifies women's bodies ... Women are not seen as human beings, but as things. Men are reared to view females in this way, pornography ... feeds it, and rape is one of the consequences."

Suppose that in one year anti-Semitic violence in the U.S. rose by 45%, and a Jew was brutally mutilated. Suppose, too, that year there had been a 300% increase in the sale of anti-Semitic magazines and videotapes. Surely, American Jews would demand an investigation of the connection between these two phenomena.

In Israel, there has been an acceleration of certain types of crimes in the past few years. During this same period, there has been a drastic increase in the dissemination of printed and visual materials glorifying certain kinds of violence.

The crimes have been assaults on girls and women. The materials are pornography. And Israeli women are beginning to speak up on the connection.

While this article is not about pornography per se, but about its proliferation in and effect on Israeli life, we should take just a sentence or two to provide a working definition: pornography means the display of people as sexual objects rather than as total, complex human beings with complex histories, presents and futures, and the reduction of such persons to easily replaceable body parts (breasts, thighs, vaginas, legs, etc.).

Pornography And Violence

Dr. John H. Court, Associate Professor of Psychology at The Finders University of South Australia, in his paper on pornography presented to the International Interdisciplinary Congress on Women (Haifa, 1981), concluded that the themes of pornography channel and direct violence to women and children. These themes include pleasure in pain, rape as rewarding, and sex as a mechanistic event which one is entitled to witness. He writes:

"An extended case, starting in 1970, has been made on the basis of very dubious data from Denmark, that sex crimes go down when pornography becomes freely available ... I remain ... convinced [on the basis of various studies] that sexual assaults are not only increasing, but that this increase is in part influenced by the themes promoted by pornography." While minor

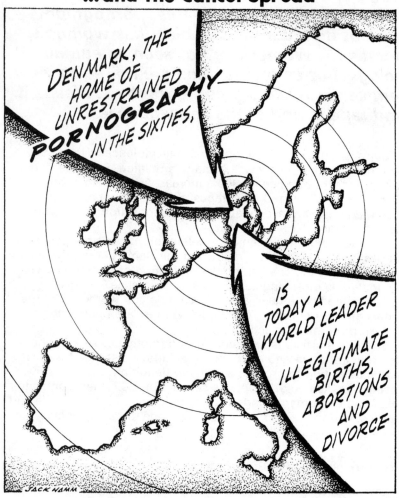

sex crime reports declined in Copenhagen, rape did not. Dr. Court writes: "In fact, the trend has been steeply up." He quotes British feminist Diana Russell:

'The point about the relationship between pornography and rape is this: pornography, even at its most banal, objectifies women's bodies ... Women are not seen as human beings, but as things. Men are reared to view females in this way, pornography ... feeds it, and rape is one of the consequences."

Israeli police statistics reveal a 45% increase in rape in Israel from 1980–1981, and a 10% increase in other sex crimes. The increase in rape cannot be explained away by the standard "more reporting" argument . . .

Moreover, the rape crisis center in Tel Aviv informs us, victims are getting younger (as in the U.S.). For the first time, parents are calling in about attacks upon children as young as five years of age . . .

My interviews with battered wives substantiate statements on the following phenomenon by Barbara Swirski of the Battered Women's Shelter in Haifa. Battering husbands (as well as emotionally and verbally abusive men), she said, commonly use pornographic photos and ideas to focus the sexual activity they force their wives into . . .

Pornography In Israel

There is considerable evidence that porn triggers rape—as well as wife battery, incest, sexual harassment on the job and other assaults on women. Is it any different from providing approval—in society to anti-Semitic or racist plays, cartoons, films, jokes? If such scope is given, anti-Semitism or racism, which is always present to some degree, will take root, grow, and become violent.

Pornography can be seen as the anti-Semitism of women. Feminists need not seek out pornography as an issue: it "finds" feminists—just as anti-Semitism finds the Jew, assimilated or not. In the same way that *Mein Kampf* was an issue for all Jews, pornography can be seen as an issue for all women.

Five years ago the incidence of pornography in Israel was lower than in the U.S. Today it is found in "legitimate" mass-circulation magazines as well as movie-house, billboard, radio and newspaper ads.

One major difference between Israeli and American pornography is that the pornographic themes of sadism, pseudo-homosexuality and child pornography are being woven into the daily family, women's and general circulation media, and the street and travel environment. Materials appear in Israeli family publications today which would still not be found in the back pages of *Playboy*. In the last few years, women's, family and youth magazines have featured advertising and "artistic" scenes which are "sensuously" brutal; in one case, sexual exploitation was combined with specifically Jewish symbols of the Holocaust.

Barely a magazine issue appears today which does not include some blatantly violent image assaulting female dignity. For example, *La Ishah,* the best-selling women's magazine in Israel, ran two suggestively-posed naked photos of Brooke Shields as an eight-year-old, next to her "grown-up" image. *Ladies' Home Journal* or any other legitimate American magazine would

107

not run a picture of a naked 15-year old girl, yet some Israeli women's and family magazines have done just that . . .

All the imported so-called soft pornography (*Playboy/Penthouse/Hustler*) is sold at newsstands everywhere, in university bookstores and by Steimatsky's, Israel's major bookstore and newsstand distributor. European pornography, and black-and-white child pornography is also available, at high prices.

The Tel Aviv bus station—supported by tax payers' money—permits porn peddlers a virtual monopoly. They have the liberty to exhibit materials floor to ceiling in the ticket-selling area. I have personally seen pictures of children in pornographic poses sold there. No other merchants have space there, only the porn peddlers.

The huge billboard film advertisements for semi- or not so semi-pornographic films are unavoidable in Tel Aviv. In Natanya in 1981, a large billboard featured a naked teenager astride an adult male, with an "older" woman looking on.

"Blue movies" are growing in fashionable chic in many social circles across the nation. In the rush to emulate sophisticated Americans and Europeans, "Deep Throat" and "The Babysitters" join a complete selection of "X" videos and films shown at private parties, and Chanukah and Purim celebrations. Even gatherings to celebrate the birth of a baby girl have been known to include "blue" movies; and, according to a colleague, in an Egged Bus Company celebration in a city building last year, Egged bus drivers and their wives disco-danced while a pornographic film was screened.

There are 100,000 video tapes in private Israeli homes, and pornographic tapes are a major sales item, according to Kol Israel Radio. One can also now order "hard-core" video tapes via local community newspaper supplements published in the daily papers. The supplements openly promote full pornographic displays, advertising the "Eros" sex shops and their sex aides . . .

Legal Restrictions

Displaying or selling pornography, "materials which incite sexual lust," is, by the way, absolutely against Israeli law, and subject to three months' imprisonment and a fine. However, as the courts, lawyers and police are still under the erroneous impression that sex crimes decreased in Denmark when pornography was legalized, they continue to view it as a trivial issue, and the law is not enforced . . .

Conclusions

Pornography did not drop from the sky: it was a well-planned, expensive effort, a concentrated marketing assault on the minds,

108

hearts, values and pocketbooks of Israelis. Millions of dollars are now earned in pornography, and merchandizers look to it and to other luxury items (stereos, fashion, liquor) for astronomical profits. In selling this *"Playboy* lifestyle" package, the Israeli communications/advertising experts understood and exploited a relatively unsophisticated population anxious to be a part of what they perceived as worldly Western culture . . .

But the *"Playboy* lifestyle" is a package deal. The growing consumption of liquor, drugs and luxuries goes hand in hand with the growth of consumption of pornography. While Israeli youth still retain an involvement, an interest, a commitment and an eager sense of humor and honor, time is not on their side. Things are moving too fast—and we are not responding to the changes adequately. Considering the high level of tension and anxiety under which the nation lives, Israel may be at grave risk from the problems triggered by pornography.

PORNOGRAPHY IN THE SOVIET UNION
Lev Annisky

Lev Annisky is a literary critic in the Soviet Union. In the following statement he presents a Soviet perspective on the nature, extent, and control of pornography in his nation.

Points To Consider

1. How is the Russian tradition described?
2. Why are Soviet people largely indifferent to pornography?
3. Why did pornography never take root?

Lev Annisky, "Why We Are Indifferent to Pornography," **Soviet Life,** July, 1978.

The point you see, lies not in the "law" or in anybody's "veto." For pornography to be a success, people have to have a need for it.

An American with whom I was discussing Soviet literature among other subjects threw me into utter confusion with the question:

"Why is pornography forbidden in your country?"

I was too bowled over at first to formulate my answer and became even more confused by my reaction to the question. In the 43 years of my life and the 20 years of my career as a literary critic, I had never given the matter a thought. Why we don't have pornography has never occurred to me. But now that I was confronted with the question, I could not help countering with: "Why *should* we have pornography? What would we do with it?"

I let myself imagine what would happen were the ban on pornography lifted, say, tomorrow.

Every morning on my way to the Metro I pass a newsstand run by an old man who tells me which papers and magazines contain the most interesting articles. Sometimes he saves a special issue of a periodical for me. I tried to imagine what he would say to me if he were officially, so to speak, allowed to sell pornography. Would he slip me a few picture postcards of ladies in scanty attire? What kind of look would he give me? I wonder.

Or, say, my school-age daughter bought something of this sort and asks me what I think about it. I'd tell her that though, on the one hand, it was crude and offensive, on the other, you "couldn't very well forbid it" and so forth. How could I look her straight in the eye?

The point, you see, lies not in the "law" or in anybody's "veto." For pornography to be a success, people have to have a need for it. But that's absurd where I'm concerned. A person must be an abstract creature, a mechanical consumer, a robot, to be affected by these artificial stimuli.

Of course, people can be turned into robots if the goal is to sell them pornography. But human beings are not made that way: *Homo sapien* has a higher nature—*human* nature . . .

Russian Tradition

The human body can hardly be considered a mystery. Ancient Greek culture, for instance, was built on the beauty of the human body and objects standing freely in space. But for the entire

Christian culture of medieval Europe, nudity was something to be concealed. The Renaissance channeled Europe and Russia in different directions. In the western part of the continent a sense of the body's splendor, its dynamism, its beauty triumphed, while in eastern Europe the old customs prevailed: The Russian icon painters cloaked the body in garments that concealed its shape, only outlining the least bit of flesh—the hand or the toe—with gilt. From the face, which was also outlined in gilt, the eyes shone, demanded and preached, subordinating and suppressing everything else. For the icon painters the body was not an object of beauty. It was a secret, a mystery—something to be cherished deeply—not to be revealed to the public eye.

In this context Pasternak's idea of the "mystery of revelation" can be understood. In this context, too, it is clear that the Russian cultural tradition does not perceive nudity in the same way as, say, Italian culture: The cherished secret is not for mass production.

I remember when, some 25 years ago—I was studying at Moscow University—a rumor spread through our department:

Pornography In Socialist Nations

It is interesting to note that in several countries where capitalism has been overthrown by workers' socialist revolutions, organized crime was driven out and pornography and the exploitation of women as prostitutes virtually eliminated. Most striking are the examples of China and Cuba. Before the revolutions in those countries, Shanghai and Havana were the "sin capitals" of their respective hemispheres; poor peasant women and children from all over the countries were forced by excruciating poverty and unemployment into prostitution—often by their own families. Since the revolutions, government policy in both countries has discouraged pornography and prostitution. In recent years, they have begun to return, at least underground.

Laura Lederer, *Take Back The Night: Women Against Pornography*, Bantam Books, 1980.

"There's a nude at the Tretyakov!" We all made a beeline for the famous gallery.

I remember that painting so well: In the snow outside the door of a heated bathhouse squats a young woman, naked, bundling her little daughter into a winter coat.

Today I regard that painting with pity. I can see the cautious timidity of that revealed nudity. The care the painter took to build the composition is obvious: You see nothing "intimate," only the back, a hip and a hand. You do not even see the face. It is covered with strands of elegant long hair. In general, everything in the painting is elegant, including the large snowflakes, through which the woman's body, hot from the bath, glows. Everything is in the painting: the traditional Siberian pride in natural health, the *boldness* of nudity—and the calculated measure of that boldness. There is everything in it but the "mystery of revelation". . .

Pornography Never Took Root

What I am trying to explain is why the exaltation of the flesh never took root in Russian culture, in Russian literature. Russian classical literature runs the gamut of love experiences. From Turgenev's touchingly fervent heroines to Dostoyevsky's fatalistic beauties, every level of happiness and tragedy can be found—everything but the *techniques* of love. There are heights of passion, but no methodology.

Pornography never took root. Even in the years of decadence prior to the Revolution of 1917, our gutter literature might have described cynical debauchery, but never "matter-of-fact sex" . . .

No, pornography did not take root . . .

"Depravity lies not in anything physical, for no manner of physical outrage amounts to depravity. Depravity—genuine depravity—lies precisely in relinquishing all moral standards .

JAPANESE PRIME TIME PORN
Lesley Rimmel

Lesley Rimmel describes the nature of pornography on national television networks in Japan. She also relates how efforts to oppose prime time pornography are being organized and compares the racism of pornography in America and Japan.

Points To Consider

1. What is the purpose of the "Machiko Sensei?"
2. How have Japanese feminists attacked pornography in the media?
3. How do producers of pornography respond to criticism?

Lesley Rimmel, "Japanese Prime Time Porn," **Women Against Pornography Newsreport,** Fall/Winter, 1983.

The parallels of this program and the comics in Playboy magazine are numerous. Both promote rape and child molestation, and both use the ridicule of working women as "entertainment" for males.

Japanese feminists are protesting a pornographic children's book and television cartoon series called "Machiko Sensei" (Miss Machiko). The comic strips—appearing monthly in *Challenging Boys* magazine (an "educational" publication very popular with elementary school boys) and in a best-selling book—and the television program, appearing at 7:30 every Thursday evening nation-wide and produced by Channel 12 of Tokyo TV, involve the activities of a young elementary school teacher, Machiko, who for the most part exists for the gratification of the sexual fantasies of boy students and male teachers.

In both the TV and magazine cartoons, the main preoccupation of the male pupils and teachers is to see up Machiko's skirt, pull off her top and touch her breasts, or watch her bathing. (One of the "themes" of the series might seem to be the promotion of cleanliness, for Machiko is constantly shown in the bath or shower, whether or not that is relevant to the story, which it rarely is.) In fact, the TV show combines "moral lessons," such as that friendship can't be bought or that one shouldn't count one's chickens before they hatch, with the promotion of voyeurism. The underlying message of both comics and TV series, however, is that even if you are an independent, athletic science teacher, as a female you can still be stripped and ridiculed by the boys.

In addition, the TV show presents Machiko—and by extension, all women—as wanting to be molested. In the weekly theme song Machiko indecisively whines "Maiiching"— dooooooonnn't—as the boys put a fan under her skirt, pull her bathing suit off with fish hooks as she swims, or catch her showering in the locker room. The boys, on the other hand, sing that they "are little devils/little devils love wickedness/success, success, success . . . we can't stop wickedness."

Two Japanese feminist groups, International Women's Year Action Organization and the ad hoc Group Protesting Machiko, organized symposia on the program, wrote letters to the major newspapers, and collected thousands of signatures to protest the television program. They argued that the show should be discontinued for several reasons. First, by presenting Machiko as physically mature but emotionally childlike, as well as agreeable

115

to molestation, the producers promote the idea that males should be aggressors and that females enjoy being passive victims. Second, the groups pointed out, "skirt-lifting" and even rape are on the rise in Japanese schools; in one case the rapist admitted to having been "stimulated" by the Machiko program. Finally, the feminists contended, the show was purposely put on the air at a time when parents are busy and children are least likely to be supervised. The groups urged parents and teachers to discourage children from watching the show.

The Producers

The producers of the show countered that "Machiko Sensei" was one of the top-rated shows of the channel, and that anyone opposing it was "deviant." In fact there was little chance the producers would look upon the protest with sympathy, for the show portrays independent, noncompliant women as mean, grotesque hags. The producers also said that "Machiko" was good for the "relaxation and relief" of the boy students, who were under great academic pressures. He did not say how girls were supposed to get relief from this program.

The parallels of this program and the comics in *Playboy* magazine are numerous. Both promote rape and child molestation, and both use the ridicule of working women as "entertainment" for males. Moreover, both *Playboy* and "Machiko" justify themselves by their efforts to include "enlightenment" (the so-called
116

good articles of *Playboy*) alongside their misogyny. Finally, both "Machiko" and *Playboy* are tinged by racism. Machiko herself and most of the other women in the TV program are Western-looking. This is in keeping with the Japanese tradition of using Westerners for adult pornography. And, of course, it corresponds with Western pornography's use of women of color. All promote the "other-ness," the "differentness," of females so as to make viewers less sympathetic to subsequent ridicule of and violence against women.

EXAMINING SEXIST STEREOTYPES

Feminist groups believe women are constantly portrayed in stereotyped ways. Increasingly women have become more concerned with the limiting and/or negative portrayal of themselves by the media. They feel the following images of women in various types of media are harmful and should be eradicated:

- *Media that depicts violence as glamorous and exciting, thereby encouraging violence against women as a desirable act.*
- *Images that glamorize the use of children as sexual objects, and teaches men that child sexual abuse, incest and child prostitution are acceptable forms of entertainment.*
- *Portrayals that reinforce and encourage stereotypic and degrading images of women of color, thereby preventing them from pursuing their individual goals and life potentials.*
- *Images that encourage women not to accept their bodies as they are but to try to change themselves in order to conform to our society's view of beauty. (i.e., weight loss, cosmetics, etc.)*
- *Portrayals of working women as sexual objects to the exclusion of their skills and capabilities. (i.e., Girl Fridays, airline attendants, etc.)*
- *Media that encourages young women to escape aging at any cost; and further encourages women to feel badly about growing older and reinforces our culture's negative attitudes towards older people (Oil of Olay, haircoloring, etc.)*
- *Images that cause women to feel 'less-than' their male counter-parts, both physically and mentally. (A Woman's special problems/needs, Because you're a woman, etc. . . .)*

Guidelines

1. Examine each statement above that describes a negative image and/or stereotype of women. Do you agree or disagree with the message of each statement? Why or why not?

2. Think about photos of women in advertising you have seen in magazines and newspapers. Do any of the stereotypes mentioned above apply to these photos?

3. Try to locate examples of negative portrayals of women in magazines and newspapers.

BIBLIOGRAPHY

MAGAZINES AND NEWSPAPERS

Bakshian, A. "Two Cheers for Rape." **National Review** (Sept. 16, 1983).

Basler, B. "Child-Pornography Ruling is Seen Acting as Deterrent." **New York Times** (July 6, 1982).

Berkowitz, Leonard. "Sex and Violence: We Can't Have it Both Ways." **Psychology Today** (Dec., 1971) pp. 14, 18–23.

Brothers, J. "Child Molesters: The Monsters Who Prey on Innocent Kids." **New York Post** (May 17, 1983).

Clark, A. E. "U.S. Prohibits Festival Screening of a Japanese Film as Obscene." **New York Times** (Oct. 2, 1976) Section 1, p. 12.

Coburn, J. "Can You Make a Case for Pornography?" **Mademoiselle** (Jan., 1982) p. 56.

Collins, G. "Sex Abuse: The Child's Word Isn't Enough," **New York Times Style** (July 11, 1983).

Dietz, Park Elliot. "Supply and Demand in Porn Market." **Psychology Today** (Mar., 1983) p. 9.

Donnerstein, Edward and John Hallan. "Facilitating Effects of Erotica on Aggression Against Women." **Journal of Personality and Social Psychology** (Sept. 1978) pp. 1270–77.

Dudar, H. "America Discovers Child Pronography." **Ms.** (Aug. 1977).

Feshbach, S. and N. Malamuth. "Sex and Aggression: Proving Link." **Psychology Today** (Nov., 1978) pp. 111–18, 122.

Fields, H. "Federal Kiddieporn Bill Changed to Meet Objectives." **Publishers Weekly** (Feb. 25, 1983) p. 23.

Fields, H. "High Court Hears New York Child Pornography Case." **Publishers Weekly** (May 14, 1982) p. 114.

Fields, H. "House Kiddieporn Bill Exempts Print Matter." **Publisher's Weekly** (Dec. 2, 1983) p. 21.

Fields, H. "McCormack Warns Hearing on Fed Child Porn Law." Testimony before Senate Judiciary Committee. **Publishers Weekly** (Dec. 24, 1982) p. 18.

Fields, H. "Senate Committee Approves Onerous Obscenity Bill." **Publishers Weekly** (Dec. 4, 1981) p. 14.

Fields, H. "Senate Kiddieporn Unit Cuts Protections." **Publishers Weekly** (May 20, 1983) p. 122.

Fields, H. "Supreme Court Upholds Kiddie Porn Law." **Publishers Weekly** (July 23, 1982) pp. 66–68.

Haskell, Molly. "The Night Porno Films Turned Me Off." **New York Magazine** (March 29, 1976) p. 56.

Hirschberg, L. "Giving Good Phone [Telephone Sex] Services." **Rolling Stone** (Dec. 22, 1983–Jan. 5, 1984) pp. 137–41.

Hirschfeld, N. "For Kid Hookers, Game is 'Trick' and Treat: Feds." **New York Daily News** (April 29, 1982).

Hluchy, P. "A Definition of Obscenity." **Macleans** (Nov. 7, 1983) p. 63.

Johnson, R. "Kiddies Star in Sodom & Gomorrah Scenes at Porn 'Sunday School'." **New York Post** (March 19, 1982).

Juffe, M. "Kid Stuff's the Hot New Trend in Fashion." **New York Post** (Nov. 22, 1982).

Juffe, M. and A. Haden-Guest. "Pretty Babies." **New York** (Sept. 29, 1980) pp. 32–37.

Krauthammer, C. "Pornography through the Looking Glass." **Time** (Mar. 12, 1984) p. 82.

Leo, J. "Cradle-to-Grave Intimacy." **Time** (Sept. 17, 1981) p. 69.

Lockhart, W. B. and R. McClure. "Censorship of Obscenity." 45 **Minnesota Law Review** 5. Pp. 62–66.

Lockhart, W. B. and R. McClure. "The Law of Obscenity." 38 **Minnesota Law Review** 295. Pp. 320–324.

Malamuth, N., M. Heim and S. Feshbach. "Sexual Responsiveness of College Students to Rape Depictions: Inhibitory and Disinhibitory Effects." **Journal of Personality and Social Psychology** (1980).

McConahay, M. J. "Antiporn Activists at San Jose." **Ms.** (Oct., 1983) p. 84.

McKinnon, Isaiah. "Child Pornography." **FBI Law Enforcement Bulletin** (Feb. 1979) pp. 18–21.

Morgan, Robin. "How to Run the Pornographers Out of Town (and Preserve the First Amendment)." **Ms.** (Nov. 1978) p. 55.

Mutter, J. "New Georgia Minors' Access Law Challenged." **Publisher's Weekly** (April 20, 1984) p. 16.

O'Connor, C. "Have a Look at Who's Teaching Your Child About Sex." **The (Hackensack) Record** (June 14, 1982).

Payton, Jennifer M. "Child Pornography Legislation." **Journal of Family Law** 17, no. 3 (1978–79) pp. 505–44.

Press, R. M. "Secrecy in Child Pornography Thwarts Law Enforcement." **Christian Science Monitor** (May 26, 1982).

Rembar, C. "Obscenity—Forget It." **Atlantic** (May, 1977) pp. 37–41.

Reuter, M. "New Action on New York Kiddie Porn Law." **Publishers Weekly** (Oct. 1, 1982) p. 33.

Rooney, R. "Children for Sale." **Readers Digest** (July, 1983) pp. 52–56.

Ross, B. "Child Rape is on Rise, Says Task Force." **New York Post** (Aug. 2, 1983).

Schultz, LeRoy G. "The Sexual Abuse of Children and Minors: A Bibliography." **Child Welfare** 58, no. 3 (1979) pp. 147–63.

Serrin, William. "Sex is a Growing Multimillion Business." **New York Times** (Feb. 9, 1981).

Steinem, G. "Is Child Pornography About Sex?" **Ms.** (Aug. 1977).

"Censorship Threat." **Publishers Weekly** (Feb. 18, 1983) p. 58.

"Civil Liberties Union Assails Smut Prosecution." **New York Times** (Dec. 16, 1976) p. 18.

"Innocence for Sale." **Ladies Home Journal** (Aug. 1983) p. 42 and (April, 1983) pp. 79–81.

"Librarians Assail Child Pornography Statute." **New York Times** (Nov. 26, 1982).

"Morgenthau Finds Film Dismembering Was Indeed a Hoax." **New York Times** (March 10, 1976).

"Most Obscenity Seized at Border Features Youths." **New York Times** (July 28, 1982).

"Prostitution Urged to Cut Welfare Roll". **Tucson Daily Citizen**. Reprinted in Ms. Magazine (Sept. 1974).

"Special Reports: Child Pornography." **Behavior Today** (May 2, 1983).

"Supreme Court Rules Against Child Porn." **Christianity Today** (Aug. 6, 1982) p. 58.

"Supreme Court Sets Lower Standard for Obscenity Test." **Publishers Weekly** (Dec. 18, 1981) p. 23.

"The Mother of Kiddie Porn?" C. Wilson Case. **Newsweek** (Jan. 23, 1984) p. 70.

"The Victim Syndrome." **The Progressive** (June, 1982) pp. 42–47.

"The Voice with the Leer: FCC Crackdown on Erotic Dial-It-Numbers." **Forbes** (Mar. 26, 1984) p. 12.

"X-Rated Films Banned from Cincinnati Cable TV." **Christianity Today** (Sept. 2, 1983) pp. 47–48.

"You Can Stop Pornography." **Readers Digest** (June, 1982) pp. 181–83.

BOOKS AND DOCUMENTS

Donnerstein, Edward. "Pornography: Its Effect on Violence Against Women." **Pornography and Sexual Aggression** (New York: Academic Press).

Dworkin, R. "Liberty and Moralism." **In Taking Rights Seriously** (Cambridge, Mass.: Harvard University Press: 1979) pp. 240–258.

Eysenck, H. J. and D.K.B. Nias. **Sex, Violence, and the Media** (London: Maurice Temple Smith; New York: St. Martin's Press, 1978).

Marcus. **The Other Victorians: A Study of Sexuality and Pornography in Mid-Nineteenth Century England** (New York: Basic Books, 1966).

Mohr, J. C. **Abortion in America: The Origins and Evaluation of National Policy, 1800–1900** (New York: Oxford University Press, 1978) pp. 196–199.

President's Commission on Obscenity and Pornography. **Report** (Washington, D.C.: Government Printing Office, 1970).

Russell, Diana E. H. "Rape, Child Sexual Abuse, Sexual Harassment in the Workplace: An Analysis of the Prevalence, Causes and Recommended Solutions". A Final Report for the California Commission on Crime Control and Violence Prevention (March, 1982) pp. 17–20.

Sarris, Andrew. **Politics and Cinema** (New York: Columbia University Press, 1978).

Schultz, LeRoy G. **"Kiddie Porn": A Social Policy Analysis** (Morgantown: University of West Virginia, 1977).

Sobel, Lester A., ed. **Pornography, Obscenity and the Law** (New York: Facts on File, 1979).

"Child Pornography." **Congressional Record**—House H3894 (June 14, 1983).

"Sexual Exploitation of Children." **Congressional Record**—Senate S10207 (July 16, 1983).

FEMINIST CRITIQUE OF PORNOGRAPHY

Armstrong, Louise. **Kiss Daddy Goodnight** (New York: Hawthorn Books, 1978).

Barry, Kathleen. **Female Sexual Slavery** (Englewood Cliffs, N.J.: Prentice-Hall, 1979).

Blakely, Mary Kay. "Who Were the Men?" **Ms.** 50 (July, 1983).

Brownmiller, Susan. **Against Our Will: Men, Women and Rape** (New York: Simon and Schuster, 1975).

Burgess, Ann W. A **Handbook on Rape Research,** "Media Violence and the Civil Rights of Women and Children; A look forward to the Future", Garland Press ★ book forthcoming.

Colker, Ruth. "Pornography and Privacy: Towards the Development of a Group Based Theory for Sex Based Intrusions of Privacy" 1, 2 **Law and Equality: A Journal of Theory and Practice (1983).**

Dworkin, Andrea. "The Root Cause", in A. Dworkin. **Our Blood: Essays and Discourses on Sexual Politics** (New York: Harper and Row, 1976).

Dworkin, Andrea. **"Pornography: Men Possessing Women** (New York: Perigree Books, 1981).

Dworkin, Andrea. **"Right-Wing Women** (Ibid.: Perigree Books, 1983).

Gould, Lois, essay in **Not Responsible for Personal Articles.**

Griffin, Susan. **Pornography and Silence** (New York: Harper and Row, 1981).

Hite, Shere. **The Hite Report on Male Sexuality** (New York, 1982) pp. 10–49.

Kotash, Myrna. "Power and Control: A Feminist View of Pornography." **This Magazine** (July–Aug. 1978) pp. 4–7.

Lederer, Laura (ed.) **Take Back the Night** (all essays, including particularly Alice Walker, "Coming Apart") (New York: Morrow [Bantam ed.] 1982).

Leidholdt, Dorchen. "Where Pornography Meets Fascism" **WIN**. March 15, 1983, pp. 18–22.

Lovelace, Linda. **Ordeal** (Seacaucus, New Jersey: Citadel Press, 1980).

MacKinnon, Catherine A. **Sexual Harassment of Working Women: A Case of Sex Discrimination** (Yale, 1979).

Millett, Kate. **Sexual Politics**. (New York: Avon Books, 1971).

Mulvey, Laura. "Visual Pleasure and Narrative Cinema," **Screen**. v. 16, No. 3, 1975.

Morgan, Robin. "Pornography and Rape", **Going Too Far**. (New York: Random House, 1977).

Reisman, Judith A. A Critical Analysis of the Kinsey Sex Research with Particular Emphasis upon the "Child Sexuality" Research Reported in **Sexual Behavior in the Human Male**, 1948. Jack Martin, Commerce Publishing, 5757 Alpha Road, Dallas, Texas 214, 2394481 ★ book forthcoming.

Russell, D., Pagano, Star and Linden, (eds), **Against Sadomasochism**. (East Palo Alto, Ca.: Frog in the Well Press, 1982).

Rush, Florence. **The Best Kept Secret: The Sexual Abuse of Children**. (New York: McGraw Hill, 1982).

Review of Law and Social Change. (New York University), Vol. 8 (1978–79).

Steinem, Gloria. "I Was a Playboy Bunny" and "The Real Linda Lovelace" in Steinem, ed. **Outrageous Acts and Everyday Rebellions** (New York: Holt, Rinehart, 1983).

Stoltenberg, John. "Sexual Objectification and Male Supremacy," **M**. Spring 1981, p. 5; " 'Good Sex' and Gay Male Pornography" **M**. (forthcoming, 1984); "The Forbidden Language of Sex" Speech Delivered at the Writer's Congress, New York, New York, 1981, available through Elaine Markson, 44 Greenwich Avenue, New York, New York 10011.

Vidal, Gore. "Women's Liberation Meets the Miller-Mailer-Manson Man" **Homage to Daniel Shays Collected Essays 1952–1972**. (New York: Random House, 1972) pp. 389–402.